The Electro-Diesels

An Illustrated History of Classes 73 and 74

Above: The launch of the revamped 1980s 'Gatwick Express' service took place on 14 May 1984. To mark the event Class 73 No 73123 was repainted in InterCity livery to match the Mk2 stock. The locomotive was also named *Gatwick Express* to coincide with the event. On the first day, a special headboard was carried, produced by the Carriage & Wagon Department at Stewarts Lane, and is shown attached to the 12.30 Victoria-Gatwick Airport service passing Clapham Junction. *Author*

Previous Page: After many years of trying to have a Class 73 repainted into near-original green livery, agreement was given in early 1993 for No 73003 (E6003) to be returned to 1960s green livery to coincide with the closure of Selhurst Level 5 Depot, the name *Sir Herbert Walker* was also applied. At the time of repainting, No E6003 was surplus to normal operating requirements, and for a short time was kept at the Mid-Hants Railway, but following introduction of the green-liveried South West Trains 'Ocean Liner' set, it became the usual motive power for this train until withdrawal. No E6003 is seen inside Selhurst Level 5 Depot. *Author*

The Electro-Diesels

Colin J. Marsden

OPC

An imprint of
Ian Allan Publishing

Contents

First published 2006

ISBN (10) 0 86093 601 5
ISBN (13) 978 0 86093 601 5

Published by Oxford Publishing Co

an imprint of Ian Allan Publishing Ltd, Hersham, Surrey KT12 4RG
Printed in England by Ian Allan Printing Ltd, Hersham, Surrey KT12 4RG

Code: 0611/B1

Visit the Ian Allan Publishing website at
www.ianallanpublishing.com

Front cover: Painted in InterCity 'Executive' livery, Class 73/2 No 73202 *Royal Observer Corps* approaches Clapham Junction on 10 April 1988, leading the 11.30 Victoria-Gatwick Airport service. In common with many of the fleet, a cast resin '73A' Stewarts Lane shed plate was fitted to the front end. *Author*

Rear cover, top: In August 2006 GBRf-operated Class 73/2 No 73208 was restored to 1960s BR rail-blue livery by staff at Stewarts Lane. The locomotive was then made available to charter operators for a short period before being repainted into standard GBRf colours. On 10 August, the locomotive was officially named *Kirsten* in a ceremony at London Victoria, before powering a GBRf staff and customer special around south London. The locomotive is seen passing Virginia Water with the launch VIP special leading sister blue-liveried ED No 73136 with Nos 73204 and 73209 in GBRf-livery on the rear. *Author*

Rear cover, bottom: Parked up in the Windsor Yard at Clapham Junction, 'Big ED' No 74010 waits to be hauled to Doncaster Works for disposal on 17 August 1978. The 10 class 74s were not the most popular locomotives with drivers, frequently failing with electronic problems. However, with 'We will miss you' message chalked on the front, it looked as if the class had at least some admirers. *Author*

Title page: The first Class 73 to sport Mainline Freight aircraft-blue colours, No 73114 *Stewarts Lane Traction Maintenance Depot* stands outside its home shed on 14 November 1994. *Author*

Introduction

The Electro-Diesel or Class 73 and 74 locomotive fleets are the most universal locomotive type ever introduced during the modern traction era, having the ability to operate from a third 'live rail' power supply or from an on-board diesel engine/generator set.

The dual power concept was first mooted by the Southern Railway in the immediate postwar years, but due to numerous problems the design was not finally sanctioned until the late 1950s. Once authorisation was given, a pilot order for six 'prototype' locomotives was placed by the British Transport Commission (BTC) for construction at Eastleigh Carriage Works. The build was a lengthy affair with the first not emerging until early 1962. After stringent testing was completed the full potential of this design could be seen.

After the six prototypes entered service the BTC authorised a production batch of 43 similar examples, thus assisting with streamlining the then Southern Region's modern traction policy. The contract for the production locomotives, which were almost identical to the prototypes, was awarded to English Electric, which sub-contracted mechanical construction to Vulcan Foundry, Newton le Willows; production locomotives were delivered between October 1965 and January 1967. All this design were to become Class 73.

The electro-diesel design was furthered with the Bournemouth electrification in the mid-1960s when a batch of 10 straight electric locomotives of SR Class HA were rebuilt into high-output or 'Big' electro-diesels classified as 'HB' or Class 74.

From their introduction until June 1993 the '73s' were allocated to Stewarts Lane in South London, except for a handful allocated to Eastleigh in 1967-68 to assist with the Bournemouth line electrification project. However, with rationalisation of traction some of the early prototype machines became spare in mid-1993, and four were transferred to the then BR Regional Railways for use on the electrified Merseyrail system. For most of their lives the Class 73 fleet operated over all the former BR Southern Region/NSE South Thames lines on passenger and freight services. For many years their passenger duties were rather restricted, with enthusiasts and photographers having to travel far and wide to capture such trains. This position changed in May 1984 when the 15min interval 'Gatwick Express' service was introduced between London Victoria and Gatwick Airport, which were powered by Class 73s.

The Class 74 fleet, which was prone to electrical problems, only had a life of around 10 years with the entire fleet being withdrawn by 1977. This was a remarkable locomotive, able to travel happily at speeds well in excess of 100mph operating under electric conditions developing 2,552hp. Sadly after withdrawal all were broken up and none survive in preservation.

With the mid-1990s privatisation of the UK railways the Class 73 fleet fell from favour; the main fleet were taken under control of the freight company EWS, which phased them out of service, while South West Trains retained one and more recently three locomotives for 'Thunderbird' use. The use of the '73s' on the Gatwick Express operation came to an end in mid-2005 following full introduction of Class 460 EMU stock.

New players came into the operating field in the late 1990s, which has led to some Class 73s being returned to front-line use, mainly for GB Railfreight (GBRf) and FM Rail. This, together with an expanding interest from the preservation movement has meant that in 2006 we can still see the electro-diesel fleets in daily operation.

This title has been produced to detail in words and pictures the development and careers of these unique dual-power locomotives. Special emphasis has been placed on detail, to ensure that as many liveries as possible have been included, and modifications shown.

I do hope that you enjoy reading and browsing through the illustrations of these unusual classes. Long may we see the dual power concept remain as part of our railway scene.

Colin J. Marsden
Dawlish
July 2006

Below: Throughout their working lives the Class 73s had regular diagrams on all three operating divisions of the former Southern Region, and more recently over the tracks of the corresponding TOUs for the freight and private sector. However, until the Gatwick Express service was inaugurated in 1984 their passenger mileage was somewhat scarce. On 19 January 1983 No 73126 passes under the now demolished Clapham Junction 'A' signalbox arriving in Clapham Yard with empty passenger stock from Waterloo. *Author*

The Electro-Diesel Concept

The first suggestion of a dual-powered locomotive for the Southern Railway came soon after the end of World War 2. During the first 40 years of the 20th century a considerable amount of electrification work had been carried out on former Southern Railway tracks, and with further extensions likely when finance permitted, steam traction could theoretically be phased out on electrified routes quickly. While the Southern Railway and subsequently the Southern Region of the BTC was keen to operate passenger services formed of unit stock, the freight side of the business would generate many problems. With an electric multiple-unit formation, power was collected by a number of third rail pick-up shoes throughout the train's length, providing bridging for gaps in the continuity of the live rail. However, if an electric locomotive was constructed with a maximum length of around 60ft, the breaks in live rail continuity could only be less than this length to ensure power was not lost.

SR technical engineers came up with a novel 'flywheel' system; the heavyweight flywheel was powered by the live rail supply when available and rotated at comparatively high speed; coupled to the flywheel was a generator which provided current for the electric traction motors. If live rail supply was lost for anything up to around 30 seconds, depending on previous road speed, the flywheel would rotate by momentum and continue to produce a power output, thus avoiding snatching when passing over live-rail gaps. While this solution to the electric locomotive problem was satisfactory on running lines, a number of operational difficulties were foreseen. 'Pick-up' freight workings, which were a prominent feature of Southern operation, would cause the greatest headache, as the presence of a 600-750V live rail in yards would be very dangerous to staff. Consideration also had to be given to the number of yards and sidings which had public and vehicular access; the presence of live rails in these locations would also be problematic. The SR also had a number of dock complexes within its operating area and these would again prove impracticable to have a live rail supply.

A further concern which faced the planners was that a large proportion of engineering and track possessions took place on the busy south London network during the night hours, at the time when most freight traffic operated. While in many cases it was possible for the engineers to clear the possession for a train movement it was not always practical to restore the traction current. Of course, in this case the flywheel system would not be suitable for this length of time and mileage to be 'off the juice'. These three major factors clearly demonstrated that the Southern, unlike other railways at the time, needed locomotives with electric capabilities as well as an auxiliary power source. At the time many people were of the opinion that a straight diesel locomotive could operate all SR non-multiple-unit services; however, as trains would be operating alongside the electric supply, it was pointless not to exploit the system to the full. It therefore became apparent that while there were identifiable uses for electric-only and diesel-only locomotives, a dual-power electric -

Above: The initial application of electric locomotive traction came to the Southern Railway in 1941 when the first of three 'booster' electrics was introduced. The pioneer member of the build, No 20001, painted in black and aluminium livery, is seen heading a Newhaven boat train in October 1950. *BR*

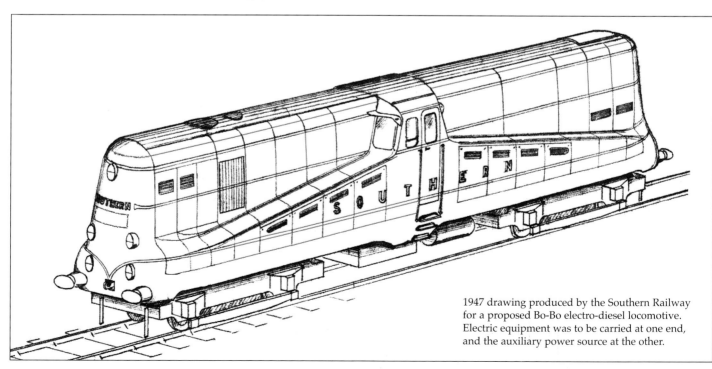

1947 drawing produced by the Southern Railway for a proposed Bo-Bo electro-diesel locomotive. Electric equipment was to be carried at one end, and the auxiliary power source at the other.

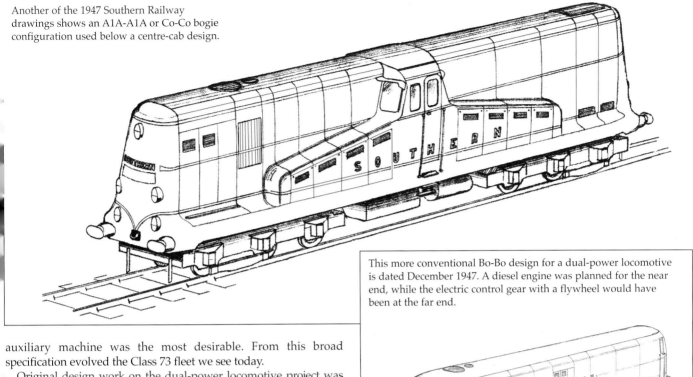

Another of the 1947 Southern Railway drawings shows an A1A-A1A or Co-Co bogie configuration used below a centre-cab design.

This more conventional Bo-Bo design for a dual-power locomotive is dated December 1947. A diesel engine was planned for the near end, while the electric control gear with a flywheel would have been at the far end.

auxiliary machine was the most desirable. From this broad specification evolved the Class 73 fleet we see today.

Original design work on the dual-power locomotive project was awarded to the Southern Railway drawing office at Brighton who took a considerable time to develop visions into structural drawings. Numerous adventurous plans were put forward, with the first practical design emerging in 1947, at which time the Southern Railway issued a directive that the locomotive should have the same output under both electric and auxiliary conditions. For this, it was proposed to use a motor generator set of the type used on the region's three electric locomotives, coupled to an 800hp diesel engine via a magnetic clutch. After numerous intermediate plans, in 1951 the designers came up with a proposition that if an independent diesel engine was provided, the generator output could be used to supplement the main electric power, however, due to very considerable wiring and power circuit complications this idea was soon dropped.

Throughout the late 1940s and early 1950s a number of different electric and auxiliary power combinations were considered. At various times submissions were put forward to obtain finance to build a dual-power prototype, but each time the BTC Board rejected the scheme, with all finance being directed to more established traction principles and the 1955 Modernisation Plan. By 1956, although with no real prospects of a prototype being authorised, the designers produced the first basically acceptable design. This was for a 54-ton locomotive carried on a Bo-Bo wheel arrangement. The starting tractive effort was projected at between 30-33,000 lbs; under electric conditions the traction output would have been around 1,200hp, with a 200hp auxiliary supply. The maximum design speed was 75mph.

The body design consisted of a central cab with narrow bonnets at each end, one nose section housing electric equipment and the other the auxiliary power source, together with brake and ancillary equipment. Although now it seems impractical to think to the contrary, no decision was made at this time that the auxiliary power source was to be a diesel engine, and considerable thought was given to the use of accumulator batteries. The output of the largest available at the time was 400 amp/hour at a five-hour rating; this would be ideal for 'pick-up' freights that required short sorties away from the

live rail, or to shunt trains of around 500-600 tons into wayside sidings. However, the potential had to be available to operate heavy trains further away from a live rail if required; this would clearly not be possible if batteries were used, and thus the diesel option became the most desirable. After the decision was made to pursue the electric-diesel option, a new basic design specification was prepared - that of a 38ft 9in long body carried on a Bo-Bo wheel arrangement, with a cab at one end only, resembling something like the later built English Electric Type 1 diesel locomotives. The calculated all-in weight of the dual-power design was to be just 59 tons; the one-hour electric rating planned was 800hp at 31mph, while the auxiliary engine output was still to be just 200hp.

During early 1957 a major study was made of Southern Region traction requirements, bearing in mind the extent of electrification and the types of trains operated. It had become clear that the passenger function required motive power for 300+ ton trains, operating at speeds of up to 75mph for prolonged periods. It also became more obvious that 'off the juice' running would prevail more than initially considered and therefore a larger auxiliary diesel engine would be required.

By mid-1957, when much more attention was being given to the dual-power locomotive project, dieselisation of the Hastings line was underway, and the advantages of using the same English Electric 4SRKT engine as the auxiliary power source were quickly seen. With the final decision soon taken on this as the secondary power source, a twin-cabbed locomotive was put forward as the final BTC design with a weight of 64 tons; however, due to the quite heavy diesel engine installed at one end, an uneven axle loading occurred - 17.5 ton at one end compared to 14.5 ton at the other. This deficiency was overcome by fitting ballast weights at the lighter end. The electrical output proposed was 1,500hp, this being produced by straight electric traction principles and not incorporating any booster or flywheel equipment. When the final drawings were prepared in 1958 the locomotive length had increased to about 60ft; however, the electric equipment (an amount of which could be underslung) and the diesel engine/generator group would only occupy around half the locomotive length, leaving some 20ft of space. It was suggested that this could be made available for luggage, but after consultation with the operating department it was deemed unsuitable, and an established locomotive principle was pursued.

A submission to construct six prototype electro-diesel locomotives was sought in early 1959, this being granted by the BTC in July the same year. By this time many detail drawings had been prepared, and the construction order was given to the railway's own Eastleigh Carriage Works, who had a long history of multiple-unit building.

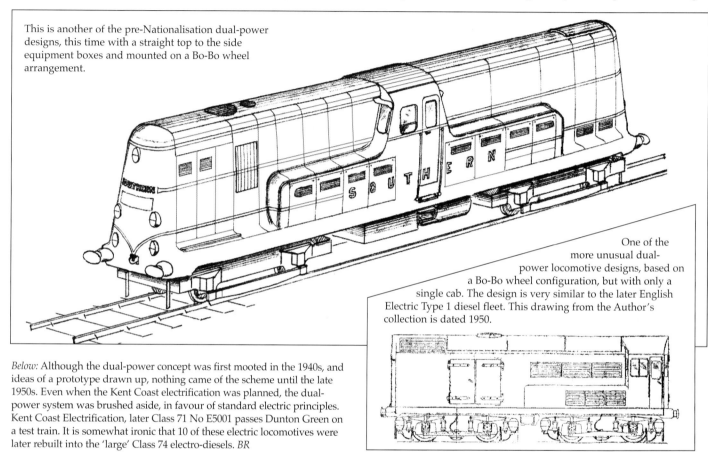

This is another of the pre-Nationalisation dual-power designs, this time with a straight top to the side equipment boxes and mounted on a Bo-Bo wheel arrangement.

One of the more unusual dual-power locomotive designs, based on a Bo-Bo wheel configuration, but with only a single cab. The design is very similar to the later English Electric Type 1 diesel fleet. This drawing from the Author's collection is dated 1950.

Below: Although the dual-power concept was first mooted in the 1940s, and ideas of a prototype drawn up, nothing came of the scheme until the late 1950s. Even when the Kent Coast electrification was planned, the dual-power system was brushed aside, in favour of standard electric principles. Kent Coast Electrification, later Class 71 No E5001 passes Dunton Green on a test train. It is somewhat ironic that 10 of these electric locomotives were later rebuilt into the 'large' Class 74 electro-diesels. *BR*

Building the Prototypes

After official agreement was granted for the construction of six prototype electro-diesels in July 1959, a number of detail drawings had to be completed; however, sufficient progress had been made for much of the steelwork to be ordered by August 1959 and a significant amount of electrical equipment during the following six weeks.

The underframe section was a fabricated structure, formed of two 12in x 6in rolled steel joists, at 2ft 0 $^3/_8$in centres running the full length between the buffer beams. Cover plates above and below the centre section made, in effect, a tube. Solebars of 7in x 3$^1/_2$in channel steel were connected to the longitudinal at the drag boxes, and transverse members, including robust stretchers at bogie centre positions were provided. In addition to transmitting the body weight to the bogies via pads, on either side of the centre line these transmitted traction and braking forces through the centre pin. The outer ends of the bogie centre stretchers were provided with lifting/jacking lugs suitable for use in lifting the body away from the bogies during maintenance, or lifting a complete locomotive in the case of a derailment. The weight differential between the diesel and electric ends of the finished product were adjusted in the buffer beams, with that at the diesel end being 3$^1/_2$in thick, while that at the lighter electric end being 6in thick. The underframe top was sealed by plates welded to the main members to prevent oil spillage.

At an early stage in the design it was agreed that the draw gear must be compatible with all post-1951 SR multiple unit and locomotive-hauled stock, therefore multiple-unit style drophead buck-eye couplers were fitted with Pullman rubbing plates above. The first three locomotives off the production line were fitted with oval style pull-out/push-in coach buffers and saddles, while the other three were fitted with 'Oleo' pneumatic buffers, which by rotating through 90deg and inserting a locking pin, could be locked in an extended or retracted position depending on the method of coupling to be used. With the buck-eye coupling used, the buffers were retracted so that end contact was passed through the centre coupling. Under conventional coupling, the buck eye would be lowered and the screw coupling used, when the buffers would be extended to take end buffing loads.

It was decided that the dual-power workhorses would be a truly universal machine, being constructed to the narrow 'Hastings' profile. The bodysides were fabricated in the form of a warren girder, the members consisting of steel sections stiffened by horizontal and vertical 'Z' sections covered on the outside by 14-gauge sheet steel. The main purpose of the body sides was to stiffen the framework and minimise vibrational deflections. The locomotive body sides were basically flat, being 8ft 2in wide at the sole bar, sloping in to 7ft 10in at the cantrail, thus conforming in all ways to the Hastings line profile and having a route availability that would permit their operation over the majority of SR lines.

The roof was of conventional coach style construction, the two central sections were formed in a translucent material and were, of course, removable to facilitate internal equipment overhaul. The body interior for the electrical compartment was panelled with thin gauge steel plate. The engine compartment walls were panelled in sheet aluminium, mainly to assist with cleanliness. The electrical resistance compartment, approximately mid-length along the body, was open at the top with only a wide-gauge wire grille providing protection; this opening giving free circulation of air to the electrical equipment. To reduce damp damage the section was formed of galvanised steel. Along the body side, there was one equipment room door on each side, together with several windows and ventilation louvres, the latter of which had vertical vein grilles on the

Below: Following the official agreement for construction of the six prototype electro-diesels in July 1959, Eastleigh Carriage Works was awarded the construction contract. Building the first machine turned out to be a lengthy process, with No E6001 not emerging until February 1962. The first 'prototype' is seen painted in multiple-unit green livery, with a small yellow warning panel and coach-style 'lion and wheel' crests, in the works yard on 2 February for its official photographs. *Author's Collection*

outermost side. Full-height cooler group grilles were positioned at the No 1 or diesel engine end, with battery boxes located at the No 2 end. The driving cabs, which were fabricated in a similar manner to the main body, were lined with thin plywood sheets onto which Formica laminate was applied. The cab roof, a one-piece structure, was moulded out of polyester resin reinforced by glass fibre and formed of an outer and inner skin with foam insulation between. The layout of the cab is described in a later section, but to provide excellent all-round visibility two forward-facing windows were provided flanking a central two-character headcode box, together with side and door drop lights. The cab floor was plated in aluminium onto which linoleum was fixed. To protect train crews from excessive engine noise, all cabs were soundproofed with the No 1 (diesel) end having special proofing material on the engine room/cab dividing bulkhead.

Bogies followed the basic mechanical principle of the type used under the SR's 2,500hp booster electric fleet of type HA, however a shorter wheelbase was used as smaller traction motors without flexible drives were incorporated; this also simplified the complete structure. The SLM-style primary suspension of the axleboxes provided good permanent lubrication of the axlebox guides and the axleboxes were easily insulated so as to carry the brushes for the 'negative' return circuit to the running rails. The bogie side members were constructed of broad flanged beams, welded in pairs to form a tubular structure. The headstocks, carrying the brake cylinders were formed of single channel steel. The complete frame was a one piece fabrication, stress-relieved and machined for the pressing in of the circular axlebox guides. The spring plank was suspended from the bogie frame by four vertical swing links 1ft $2^{1}/_{4}$ in long, given knife-edge pivots. The bolster was supported from the sprung plank by a nest of coil springs at each end. Lateral movement of the bolster relative to the bogie frame was restricted to $1^{1}/_{2}$ in by means of rubber stops. The secondary springs were centred in line with the swing links at 3ft on either side of the longitudinal bogie centre line, providing roll stability.

The main bogie springs were formed of chrome-vanadium steel which were shot peened after coiling and heat treatment. The traction links were 2ft $2^{1}/_{2}$ in long, and transmitted traction and braking loads

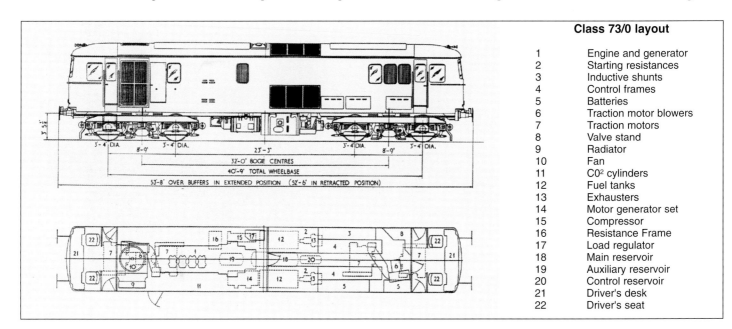

	Class 73/0 layout
1	Engine and generator
2	Starting resistances
3	Inductive shunts
4	Control frames
5	Batteries
6	Traction motor blowers
7	Traction motors
8	Valve stand
9	Radiator
10	Fan
11	CO_2 cylinders
12	Fuel tanks
13	Exhausters
14	Motor generator set
15	Compressor
16	Resistance Frame
17	Load regulator
18	Main reservoir
19	Auxiliary reservoir
20	Control reservoir
21	Driver's desk
22	Driver's seat

Right: Although the first of the six prototypes emerged in February 1962 the delivery of the remaining five was a protracted affair taking nine months to complete. No E6003, sporting revised paintwork compared to the first of the build, without the yellow warning end but with a grey solebar band, stands in company with a BRCW 'Crompton' Type 3 in Eastleigh Works yard on 27 July 1962. Note the sandboxes on the bogies. *Colin Boocock*

from the bogie frame to the bolster via brackets and rubber-mounted bushes. The actual locomotive body resting on the bogie through pads having spherical top surfaces and flat lower sliding surfaces.

Primary damping was achieved by loaded friction pads, acting with each primary spring, while secondary damping was provided by hydraulic dampers, linking the bolster and the spring plank. The locomotive wheels had rolled steel centres with separate tyres, secured by gibson rings. Braking was achieved by friction blocks, four applied to each wheel; each wheels brake being controlled by a separate brake cylinder fixed to the bogie headstock. In addition to the automatic brake equipment, handbrakes were provided in each cab which, when applied, operated on one set of wheels on the adjacent bogie. When the locomotives were designed it was not intended to install sanding equipment; however, by the time No E6003 emerged a pneumatic sanding system had been incorporated for comparative tests. The installation of such equipment considerably improved adhesion under difficult rail conditions, and in due course sanding was installed on all six prototypes.

As these primarily electric locomotives would be required to operate away from electrified areas, in localities where shoe clearances would not normally be maintained, retractable shoes were installed. The operation of the shoes was by air pressure either from the locomotive's own air compressors or by a foot pump. With no air pressure the shoes lift automatically by spring pressure. Two pick up shoes were fitted to each side of both bogies.

The Power Equipment

Electric: The majority of electric power and control equipments were supplied by the English Electric Co (EE), this consisted of basic 'straight' electric traction equipment, comparable with a modern electric multiple unit. Most power equipment was carried in equipment frames at the No 2 or electric end of the locomotive. In each driving cab the power controller governed the rate of acceleration with various manual notch-up and automatic run-up settings; movement of the power controller master switch also changes the traction motor grouping from a series to parallel or weak field group.

Diesel: The auxiliary power unit selected for use in the six prototype electro-diesels was the English Electric 4SRKT developing 600hp, this being almost identical to those installed in the SR diesel-electric multiple-unit stock. Coupled to the power unit was an

English Electric type 824/3D main generator which, when in use, gives traction current to four English Electric-supplied traction motors. To meet safety requirements an automatic CO_2 fire system was installed in the diesel compartment, activating if engine room temperature reached a pre-set level.

The English Electric traction motors were of the EE542A type, one carried by each wheel set. The motors were four-pole machines with

Below: Prior to delivery, Stewarts Lane Depot, London was deemed to be the fleet's home shed; however, when the 'new' locomotives were released from Eastleigh Carriage Works much testing was needed, and the locomotives were stabled at Eastleigh Depot for this work. Standing over one of the illuminated inspection pits at Eastleigh, No E6001 takes a rest between trials on 19 February 1962. *Les Elsey*

a one hour rating of 400hp at 675V. The motors were nose-suspended axle-hung machines with roller suspension bearings of the same type used on the majority of SR multiple unit trains. The axles were driven through spur gears with a ratio of 17:63 thus providing a top speed of 80mph, with a traction motor armature rotation speed of 2,556 rpm. An amount of technical equipment was carried between the bogies, consisting of two fuel tanks, each of 170 gallons capacity, an air compressor, auxiliary motor generator, vacuum exhausters and air reservoirs.

The electro-diesels were fitted with both air and vacuum brake equipment for trains, and a straight air brake system for the locomotive. In addition to the air/vacuum brake, an electro-pneumatic (EP) system was installed, enabling the locomotives to operate with 1951, 1957, 1963 and 1966- type EMU stock. All driving controls, including the brake valves, were duplicated on each side of the cab, this facility being very useful when shunting manoeuvres were undertaken. To simplify the driving procedure the brake controller was arranged so that the handle moved over the same rotational section whether air/vacuum or EP braking was in use. An anti-slip brake was also provided, operated by a desk-mounted

push-button, which, when depressed applied a small amount of straight air brake on the locomotive. The 'dead man's handle' or driver's safety device (DSD) was provided by foot-depressed buttons and if released initiated a full brake application after a short delay, the severity of which depended on the position of a passenger/goods brake timing switch.

An electric train heating system (ETH), later known as the electric train supply system was installed, available at all times when the locomotive is operated under electric conditions. However, under diesel conditions, train heating was only available with the master controller at the off position, *ie* when no traction power was required.

The construction of the first locomotive, numbered E6001, was a protracted affair as minor construction problems were overcome; however, painted in a distinctive livery of multiple-unit green with a small yellow warning panel, the first locomotive emerged from shops on 5 February 1962, the remaining five examples taking to the rails over the following nine months. Once the six locomotives had been released from Workshop Division control they were allocated to Stewarts Lane Electric Depot and commenced evaluation running together with driver and fitter training.

Left: Sporting coach-type oval buffers, No E6003 is seen on one of its early freight trials in Kent, powering a rake of coal hoppers at the Central Electricity Generating Board's plant at Richborough. *Author's Collection*

Below: The first time an electro-diesel operated on BR tracks was on 5 February 1962, when No E6001 hauled a six coach plus one van formation weighing 215 tons between Eastleigh Yard and Basingstoke and return. As no third rails existed west of Pirbright Junction at this time the run had to be on diesel power. It was not until the end of the month when the machine went to Stewarts Lane did the first tests under electric conditions take place. The return of the historic first run is seen near Basingstoke. *R. Puntis*

The 'JAs' in service

Right: The outward leg of the inaugural test train headed by No E6001 passes Winchester City Station on 5 February 1962. Although the engine installed in the EDs was of the same as that used in the 'Hastings' and 'Hampshire' units, the majority of technical equipment was new to railway engineers, and thorough testing had to be carried out. *R. Puntis*

Below: Looking immaculate, No E6001 approaches Basingstoke on 6 March 1962 with a test run from Woking to Eastleigh, to establish performance of the diesel engine. *Author's Collection*

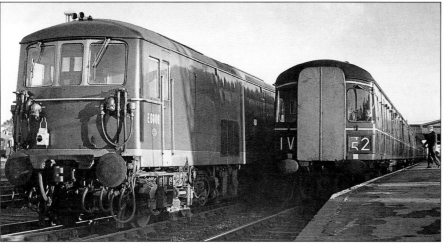

Above: During the mid-1960s the six prototype electro-diesels were tested on a number of passenger and freight duties, involving both vacuum- and air-braked services. From early 1964, a number of Kent coal trains were taken over by the fleet. These included services from the Kent coalfields and trains bringing coal into the CEGB generating station at Richborough. Electro-Diesel No E6003 propels a long train of floor discharge hoppers through the offloading equipment at Richborough Power Station on 18 March 1964. *BR*

Left: With the electro-diesels' unique facility of being able to operate at the remote ends of post-1951 EMU stock, a number of trial and training trips were operated at various locations. Further trials were carried out following agreement on the Bournemouth electrification which called for a modified push-pull system to be developed. Numerous test runs were operated with 1963-design EMUs simulating the proposed REP/TC formations, the ED taking the place of the REP. One such train, formed of No E6006 propelling CIG EMU stock, is seen at Fareham on 26 September 1965 passing an Inter-City DMMU forming the 17.27 Portsmouth Harbour-Cardiff General. *John Bird*

Left: No E6001, looking rather the worse for wear, stands outside Feltham Depot on 4 February 1967. *J. R. Menday*

Above: By 1966 when some of the new Bournemouth line TC stock was available, a number of test and training trips were operated, with the electro-diesel taking the place of the REP unit. ED No E6004 leads two 3TC sets on the South West main line in autumn 1966. *G. P. Cooper*

Middle right: When introduced, three locomotives of the prototype batch were fitted with oval 'saddle' type buffers, similar to those on conventional hauled stock. However, after a short period it was agreed to fit 'Oleo' retractable buffers as standard. These could be altered from a 'retracted' to 'extended' position by the removal of a locking pin, and turning the buffer head through 90deg. 'Oleo' fitted No E6004 is seen heading a van train near Ashford, Kent. The third rail pick-up shoes are in the raised position, indicating that the locomotive was operating under diesel conditions. *BR*

Right: In 1962/3 the Southern, South Eastern main line was host to a number of special services hauled by the new electro-diesels. Several trips were run for the benefit of the electrical engineers, who were testing on-board equipment, while others were operated for driver training purposes, as prior to their introduction the majority of main-line drivers were only familiar with steam traction. A special 'high speed' test train formed of electro-diesels Nos E6004/03, seven locomotive-hauled coaches and a MLV multiple-unit vehicle climb towards Bickley Junction on 28 September 1962. In the return direction this test train was led by the MLV; power and control over the EDs was by special train wires laid through the coaches. *Stan Creer*

Above: Displaying Southern Region EMU green livery, without a yellow warning panel, No E6003 hauls trailer set No 700, made up of redundant EMU stock past Haywards Heath on 7 September 1965 forming a driver's training special from New Cross Gate to Ore and return. *John Scrace*

Below: The brake equipment installed on the EDs was, to say the least, complicated, having the facility to convert electro-pneumatic brake signals received from the remote cab of a post-1951 EMU into a proportional vacuum or air-brake application. This enabled a train to be formed of an EMU set at the front, an Electro-Diesel sandwiched in the middle and a vacuum-braked train at the rear. Although this type of operation was seldom used, the facility remained available throughout the life of the ED fleet on the main line under the BR banner. ED No E6006, led by a 4CEP EMU, hauls Bulleid vacuum-braked passenger stock near Bickley Junction on 6 February 1964, forming a drivers' training special. *Stan Creer*

Right: Hauling a splendid loose-coupled freight train, a sight that has long disappeared from our railways, No E6005, painted in BR corporate rail blue livery with full yellow ends, passes Wandsworth Common on 9 May 1972. A few months later this locomotive was renumbered to 73005 under the BR TOPS system. *John Scrace*

Middle: For many years in the 1970s and 1980s a number of weed-control trains were operated, in an attempt to stem the flourishing weed population that infests the railway system. One of the country's main bases for weed-control trains for many years was Horsham, where Chipman Ltd had a private siding. Until the late 1980s Chipmans trains, manned and maintained by their staff, were powered and driven by BR. Pioneer ED No E6001 is seen propelling a Chipman weed control train near Warnham on 7 April 1973. Propelling of these trains was later stopped, as the driver, when looking from the side of the locomotive, could get weedkiller in his eyes. *John Scrace*

Below: With a rake of Network SouthEast-liveried stock behind, 'JA' No 73005 *Mid Hants–Watercress Line* eases out of Southampton Eastern Docks towards Northam Junction on 28 July 1990 with empty stock bound for Eastleigh after forming a charter special from Kensington Olympia to the Docks. *Brian Beer*

Above: With 'Networker' Class 465/2 No 465237 in the adjacent siding, Class 73/0 No 73001 emerges from road eight at Clapham Yard on 8 January 1993 after shunting stock into the shed off an Exeter-Waterloo service. Following the demise of locomotive-hauled West of England line services from mid-1993, the locomotive requirement at Clapham Junction was eliminated. *Brian Morrison*

Below: The repainted green-liveried 'JA' No E6003 *Sir Herbert Walker* powered only a few passenger trains over the National Network. Its first outing was on 12 April 1993 when it hauled 4TC units Nos 410 and 417 as the 10.00 London Bridge-Portsmouth Harbour Selhurst Depot staff special. The train is seen on the down main line at Earlswood complete with ceremonial headboard. *Brian Morrison*

Right: During 1994, South West Trains and Sea Containers introduced the 'Ocean Liner Express' (OLE) train, painted in green livery. Converted at Stewarts Lane, the train was available for hire and was often powered by the matching green-liveried No E6003. The first commercial outing for the OLE was on 4 May 1994 when it formed a 10.27 special from Clapham Junction to Southampton Eastern Docks, seen here awaiting departure from Clapham Junction. *Brian Morrison*

Below: The first main line trip for the restored green-liveried ED No E6003 *Sir Herbert Walker* was empty stock from Clapham Yard to London Bridge to form the Selhurst staff special to Portsmouth on 12 April 1993. The ECS move, formed of 4TCs Nos 410 and 417, is seen passing Brockley *en route* to London Bridge. *Brian Morrison*

Production Fleet - The 'JBs'

In under nine months from the emergence of the first Eastleigh prototype, the JA class, as they were classified by the SR, had created such an impression on the operators with their versatility that by late 1962 authorisation was sought to increase the fleet size. Discussions continued until June 1963 when an order for 30 'production' locomotives was placed; this was followed a few months later by a follow-on order for 13, giving a total of 43 locomotives, classified by the Southern as 'JB'. Instead of the building contract being awarded to the British Transport Commission Workshops Division, it was placed direct with English Electric (EE), who were of course the prime sub-contractor to the prototype fleet; this decision, however, caused much despondency amongst the region's workshop staff.

Physical construction of the production fleet was carried out at the English Electric Vulcan Foundry in Newton le Willows. Building methods used were very similar to those adopted for the six Eastleigh locomotives, except for a few detail revisions. The bogies were of the latest MkVI type, which was a 1964 design based on electric multiple-unit technology. The traction motors were also of a slightly different type, with revised gearing, and thus not interchangeable with the prototype fleet. The MkVI bogies were given a maximum speed of 90mph.

The internal layout and equipment was basically the same as on the JAs except for minor positioning revisions, updated wiring and redesigned panelling. Cabs were again almost identical with only minor revisions, including desk indicators and switch gear, which was brought up to date using 'Dowty' indicators in place of lamps.

On the outside of the production locomotives, most doors, windows, and louvres were in the same positions as on the prototypes, except for an alteration of the louvre position on the 'B' side, and the removal of a window panel from behind the cab on the 'A' side at No 1 end. Nose-end equipment was slightly amended, Oleo retractable buffers being fitted as standard in place of the 'saddle' type on some JAs, while one of the EMU control jumpers, fitted under the driver's-side front window was omitted. Between-bogie fittings were also revised, with a redesign of the fuel tank, motor generator and brake equipment.

Initially train crews preferred the prototype locomotives, but as experience with the English Electric fleet was acquired the benefits of the revised equipment became apparent; in later years the majority of drivers have preferred to handle the production fleet, finding these better to operate and more comfortable to work on.

The first production JB locomotive was completed at Vulcan Foundry and taken into capital stock at Stewarts Lane in October 1965.

Above: By the time the first production or English Electric ED emerged, a number of revisions were incorporated, not only to the technical side, but to the cosmetic appearance. When No E6007 was released it was painted in 'Electric Blue', with a light grey solebar band, small yellow warning panels, and a light grey roof. No E6007 is shown in the yard at EE Vulcan Foundry just prior to delivery to BR.
Author's Collection

Right: Rooftop view showing the English Electric 4SRKT engine in position. The square opening in the roof at the far end is where the cooler group fan will be positioned, while the two openings in the foreground are where electrical resistance frames are to be located. A removable roof would later be installed over the power unit area to facilitate maintenance.
GEC

Left: General view inside the EE Vulcan Foundry main erecting shop, showing five of the class under various stages of construction. This illustration clearly shows the building technique, with the nearest example showing its side frame channel girder members in position. The light centre section is made from galvanised steel to reduce damp ingress as this section is left open at the top.
GEC

Technical Specification

	Class 73/0 & 73/9	Class 73/1 & 73/2
SR classification:	JA	JB
BR classification:	72, amended to 73/0	73/1, 73/2
Original number series:	E6001-E6006	E6007-E6049
TOPS number series:	73001-73006	73/1 - 73101-73142
		73/2 - 73201-73213, 73235
Built by:	BR Eastleigh	English Electric Vulcan Foundry
Wheel arrangement:	Bo-Bo	Bo-Bo
Length over buffers (extended):	53ft 8in	53ft 8in [1]
(retracted):	52ft 6in	52ft 6in
Width:	8ft 8in	8ft 8in
Height:	12ft 0$\frac{1}{2}$in	12ft 0$\frac{1}{2}$in
Bogie centres:	32ft 0in	32ft 0in
Bogie wheelbase:	8ft 9in	8ft 9in
Total wheelbase:	40ft 9in	40ft 9in
Wheel diameter (new):	3ft 4in	3ft 4in
Weight in working order:	75ton 3cwt	77ton 1cwt
Minimum curve negotiable:	4 chains	4 chains
Nominal supply voltage:	650-750V dc	650-750V dc
Maximum speed:	80mph	90mph
Sanding equipment:	Pneumatic	Pneumatic
Heating equipment:	Electric index 66	Electric index 66
Route availability:	6	6
Multiple restriction (locomotive):	Blue star	Blue star
Multiple restriction (EMU):	27 Wire (post-1951 EMU)	27 Wire (post-1951 EMU)
Number of traction motors:	4	4
Traction motor gear ratio:	63:17	61:19
Traction motor type:	EE542A	EE546-1B
One hour rating of traction motor:	400hp	400hp
One hour rating (electric):	1,600hp	1,600hp
Traction motor mounting:	Axle hung	Axle hung
Number of field diverts:	4	4
Max tractive effort (electric):	42,000lb	40,000lb
(diesel):	34,000lb	36,000lb
Control voltage:	110V	110V
Control air pressure:	70lb/sq in	70lb/sq in
Brake type - locomotive:	Straight Air, Auto Air, EP	Straight Air, Auto Air, EP
Brake type - train:	Auto air, vacuum, EP	Auto air, vacuum *, EP
Number of brake cylinders:	8	8
Diameter of brake cylinders:	8in	8in
Brake force:	31 ton	31 ton
Air compressor type:	Metcalfe-Oerlikon 2A.115	Metcalfe-Oerlikon 2A.115
Vacuum exhauster type:	2 x Reavell FRU5	2 x Reavell FRU5 *
Number of power collector shoes:	8	8
Collector shoe base:	35ft 6in	35ft 6in
Battery cells:	48	48
Diesel engine type:	EE 4SRKT	EE 4SRKT
One hour rating:	600hp	600hp
Main generator type:	EE824/3D	EE824/5D
Main generator rating:	387kW, 850Amp	387kW, 850Amp
Auxiliary generator type:	EE908/3C	EE908/5C
Auxiliary generator rating:	29.7kW, 270Amp	29.7kW, 270Amp
Motor generator type:	EE765A	EE765A
Motor generator rating:	24kW	24kW
Fuel tank capacity:	340gal	310gal

*   Vacuum brake equipment isolated and later removed on Class 73/2 locomotives
[1] Not Nos 73118/130, which are fitted with modified Eurostar-compatible drawgear

BR 1957 No.	TOPS No.	Date Re No.	TOPS Re No.	Date Re No.
E6001	73001	02/74	73901	11/95
E6002	73002	02/74	-	-
E6003	73003	02/74	-	-
E6004	73004	02/74	-	-
E6005	73005	02/74	-	-
E6006	73006	02/74	73906	10/96
E6007	73101	01/74	-	-
E6008	73102	02/74	73212	02/88
E6009	73103	02/74	-	-
E6010	73104	03/74	-	-
E6011	73105	01/74	-	-
E6012	73106	01/74	-	-
E6013	73107	02/74	-	-
E6014	73108	01/74	-	-
E6015	73109	01/74	-	-
E6016	73110	02/74	-	-
E6017	73111	02/74	-	-
E6018	73112	03/74	73213	07/96
E6019	73113	01/74	73211	02/88
E6020	73114	02/74	-	-
E6021	73115	02/74	-	-
E6022	73116	02/74	73210	02/88
E6023	73117	01/74	-	-
E6024	73118	02/74	-	-
E6025	73119	02/74	-	-
E6026	73120	04/74	73209	02/88
E6027	-	-	-	-
E6028	73121	01/74	73208	02/88
E6029	73122	01/74	73207	02/88
E6030	73123	01/74	73206	02/88
E6031	73124	04/74	73205	02/88
E6032	73125	02/74	73204	02/88
E6033	73126	01/74	-	-
E6034	73127	01/74	73203	02/88
E6035	73128	02/74	-	-
E6036	73129	02/74	-	-
E6037	73130	02/74	-	-
E6038	73131	01/74	-	-
E6039	73132	01/74	-	-
E6040	73133	01/74	-	-
E6041	73134	02/74	-	-
E6042	73135	02/74	73235	04/91
E6043	73136	02/74		
E6044	73137	02/74	73202	02/88
E6045	73138	02/74	-	-
E6046	73139	03/74	-	-
E6047	73140	01/74	-	-
E6048	73141	02/74	-	-
E6049	73142	01/74	73201	02/88

Left: The number 73801 was applied to No 73101 for just a few hours on 25 July 1989 after the Civil Engineers decreed that locos operated by them were to be numbered in the Class 73/8 series. The numbering system had not been agreed, and the locomotive reverted to its original identification. It is seen at Clapham Junction. *Brian Morrison*

	Date named	Built by	Works No.	Date Introduced	Depot of allocation	Present Status	Operator	Date Withdrawn	Notes
	-	BR Eastleigh	-	02/62	73A	Preserved	Dean Forest	05/00	
	-	BR Eastleigh	-	03/62	73A	Preserved	Dean Forest	11/95	
rbert Walker	03/93	BR Eastleigh	-	04/62	73A	Preserved	Great Central	09/96	
luebell Railway	09/87-09/90	BR Eastleigh	-	07/62	75D	Broken up	-	03/91	Cut up, EMR 02/04
ants - cress Line	09/88-07/93	BR Eastleigh	-	07/62	75D	Preserved	Severn Valley	06/01	
	-	BR Eastleigh	-	11/62	75D	Preserved	Severn Valley	06/01	
on Evening Argus Royal Alex'	12/80-04/92 05/92	EE.VF	3569/E339	10/65	75D	Preserved	Dean Forest	05/02	No 73100 03-30/12/80 only No 73801 25/07/89 only
r Suisse	04/85-04/89	EE.VF	3570/E340	10/65	75D	Operational	Network Rail	-	
	-	EE.VF	3571/E341	11/65	75D	Stored	FM Rail	01/99	Stored Meldon Quarry
	-	EE.VF	3572/E342	11/65	75D	Stored	FM Rail	06/02	Stored Mid-Hants Railway
rant	11/87-08/89	EE.VF	3573/E343	12/65	75D	Stored	FM Rail	07/01	Stored Battlefield Line
	-	EE.VF	3574/E344	12/65	75D	Broken up	-	02/00	Cut up, Booths 09/04
ll 1844-1994 e	04/94-10/99 09/04	EE.VF	3575/E345	12/65	75D	Operational	FM Rail	-	
	-	EE.VF	3576/E346	01/66	75D	Broken up	-	01/02	Cut up, Booths 09/04
of Britain Anniversary	09/90	EE.VF	3577/E347	01/66	75D	Operational	SWT	-	Named Force O Weymouth 07-29/07/94 only
	-	EE.VF	3578/E348	01/66	75D	Preserved	Churnet Valley	05/02	
	-	EE.VF	3579/E349	01/66	75D	Broken up	-	05/91	Cut up, MRJ Phillips 01/97 at SL
rsity of Kent nterbury	04/90-08/99	EE.VF	3580/E350	02/66	75D	Operational	Network Rail	-	
ty of West ex	07/86-04/91	EE.VF	3581/E351	02/66	75D	Stored	Private	08/04	Stored Stewarts Lane
arts Lane Traction enance Depot	11/94-04/99	EE.VF	3582/E352	02/66	75D	Stored	FM Rail	12/00	Stored Battlefield Line
	-	EE.VF	3583/E353	02/66	75D	Broken up	-	04/82	Cut up, Selhurst 05/82
urst	09/86-08/99	EE.VF	3584/E354	03/66	75D	Stored	Private	08/04	Stored Stewarts Lane
rsity of Surrey	07/87-05/03	EE.VF	3585/E355	03/66	75D	Stored	FM Rail	01/99	Stored Meldon Quarry
Romney Hythe ymchurch Railway	05/87-09/94	EE.VF	3586/E356	03/66	75D	Operational	EPS	-	Fitted with Scharfenberg couplers
sh Mercury	08/86-01/99	EE.VF	3587/E357	03/66	75D	Preserved	Keith & Dufftown	-	
n	10/04	EE.VF	3588/E358	04/66	75D	Operational	GBRf	-	
	-	EE.VF	3589/E359	04/66	75D	Broken up	-	07/72	Cut up, BR Slade Green
don 1883-1983	09/83-08/99	EE.VF	3590/E360	04/66	75D	Operational	GBRf	-	
ty of East Sussex	07/85-08/99	EE.VF	3591/E361	04/66	75D	Stored	GBRf	07/03	Stored GBRf Peterborough
ick Express	05/84-08/99 10/04	EE.VF	3592/E362	05/66	75D	Operational	GBRf	-	
on Chamber of merce ette	06/87-12/94 10/04	EE.VF	3593/E363	05/66	75D	Operational	GBRf	-	
arts Lane 1860-1985 e	09/85-08/99 10/04	EE.VF	3594/E364	05/66	75D	Operational	GBRf	-	
& East Sussex ay	05/91	EE.VF	3595/E365	05/66	75D	Stored	Cotswold Rail	01/99	Stored Moreton-in-Marsh
	-	EE.VF	3596/E366	05/66	75D	Stored	GBRf	07/03	Stored GBRf Peterborough
S. Bulleid CBE	09/91-07/96	EE.VF	3597/E367	06/66	75D	Preserved	Chasewater Rly	02/02	
of Winchester	12/82-07/02	EE.VF	3598/E368	06/66	75D	Preserved	GW Railway	06/02	
of Portsmouth	07/88-06/93	EE.VF	3709/E369	07/66	75D	Operational	EPS	-	Fitted with Scharfenberg couplers
ty of Surrey	03/88-09/93	EE.VF	3710/E370	07/66	75D	Broken up	-	09/03	Cut Booths 08/04
	-	EE.VF	3711/E371	07/66	75D	Stored	HNRC	09/03	Stored RTC Derby
Bluebell Railway	09/90-09/04	EE.VF	3712/E372	08/66	75D	Preserved	Vale of Glamorgan	12/03	
ng Homes -1985	10/85-04/99	EE.VF	3713/E373	08/66	75D	Stored	FM Rail	04/99	Stored Meldon Quarry (in use on Dartmoor Railway)
	-	EE.VF	3714/E374	08/66	75D	Operational	SWT	-	
Youth Music everance	05/92-04/02 07/05	EE.VF	3715/E375	09/66	75D	Operational	Private/GBRf	-	
al Observer Corps e Berry	10/85-08/99 07/05	EE.VF	3716/E376	09/66	75D	Operational	Gatwick Express	-	
Haste - 150 s of Travelling Offices	05/88-06/90	EE.VF	3717/E377	10/66	75D	Preserved	Barrow Hill	10/99	
	-	EE.VF	3718/E378	10/66	75D	Stored	FM Rail	07/01	Stored Mid-Hants Railway
	-	EE.VF	3719/E379	10/66	75D	Preserved	Spa Valley Rly	11/98	
	-	EE.VF	3720/E380	12/66	75D	Stored	Network Rail	07/01	Stored York Works
dlands	09/80-04/99	EE.VF	3721/E381	01/67	75D	Operational	SWT	-	

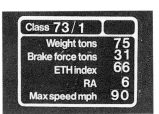

Class 73/1	
Weight tons	75
Brake force tons	31
ETH index	66
RA	6
Max speed mph	90

Left: Standard locomotive data panel of 1970s stick-on style as applied to No 73108.

Right: 1974-applied white stick-on TOPS numbers applied to No 73108. Note behind, the original 'E' number can be seen. *Both: Author*

To assist model enthusiasts and those interested in locomotive detail, this section takes a look at the equipment positions both internal and external on the Class 73/1 type, equipment positions are similar on the Class 73/0.

The front illustration identifies all major components, while the two side views show both sides of the locomotive giving the main equipment positions.

In the 1990s to reduce maintenance costs, the vacuum brake equipment was removed from the Class 73/2s, the underframe mounted exhauster have been taken off, as well as the bufferbeam vacuum pipe and pipework.

A single Group Standard headlight was centrally mounted on the front ends from mid-1990.

Gatwick Express-operated No 73202 has more recently been fitted with a bodyside door release light for operation with Juniper Class 460 stock.

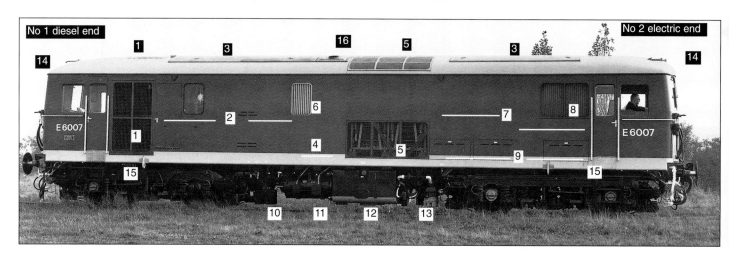

Above & Below: Class 73/1 equipment positions. *Above,* left side of No E6007 in as-built electric-blue livery; *below,* right side of No 73102, showing 1980s BR Executive colours. Both: *Author.* 1 - Coolant group with roof mounted fan, and side radiators, 2 - Position of power unit, centrally mounted, 3 - Removable fibreglass roof sections, 4 - Position of main and auxiliary generators, 5 - Starting resistances, 6 - Air intake for diesel engine, 7 - Electrical equipment, either side of central walkway, 8 - Air intake for traction motor blower, 9 - Battery boxes, 10 - AWS receiver, 11 - Motor generator set, 12 - Fuel tank, 13 - Vacuum exhauster, 14 - Two tone air warning horns. 15 - Body lifting points, 16 - Diesel engine exhaust and silencer, 17 - Bogie arc guards.

Right: Class 73/1 front end layout, showing 1980s condition before headlights were installed:
1 - Two-tone air warning horns, 2 - High level multiple control jumper cable, 3 - High level multiple control jumper receptacle, 4 - High level air brake pipe, 5 - High level main reservoir pipe, 6 - Pullman rubbing plate, 7 - Diesel air control pipe, 8 - ETS jumper socket, 9 - ETS jumper cable, 10 - Diesel control jumper socket (cable kept in engine room), 11 -Vacuum pipe, 12 - Buckeye coupling, 13 - Air brake pipe, 14 - Main reservoir pipe. The locomotive shown is No 73123 *Gatwick Express. Author*

Below: Class 73/1, 73/2 bogie detail:
1 - Bogie arc shields (original type Class 73/2), 2 - Third-rail power pick-up shoes (retracted position), 3 - Axle box, 4 - Sand box, 5 - Primary suspension, 6 - Bolster vertical damper, 7 - Traction arm, 8 - Locomotive body lifting point, 9 - Cab footsteps. *Author*

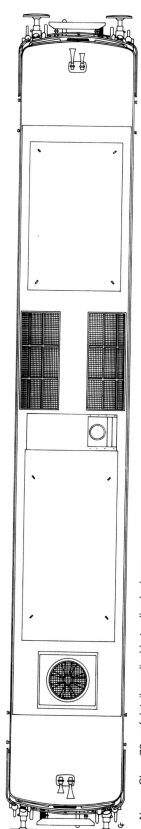

Above: Class 73 roof detail. applicable to all sub-classes

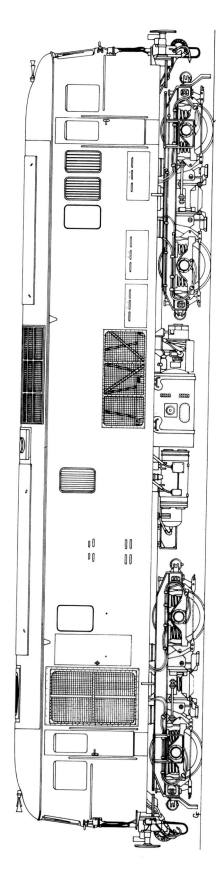

Above: Class 73/0 side elevation - as built without sand boxes.

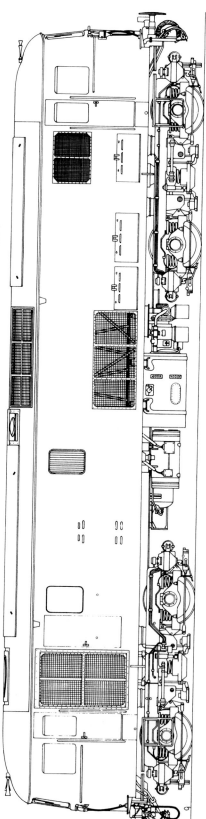

Above: Class 73/1 side elevation - No 1 end to left.

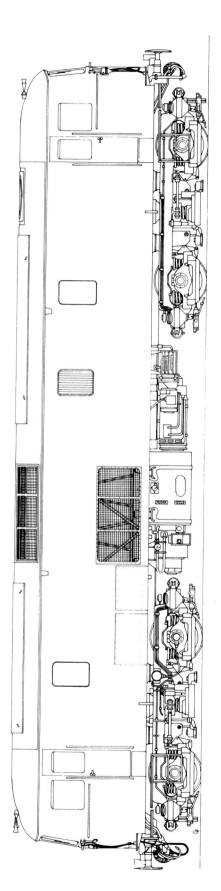

Above: Class 73/1 side elevation - No 1 end on right.

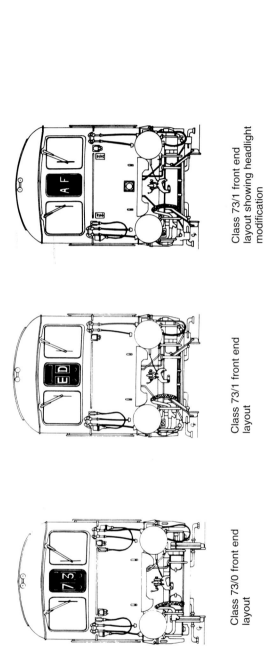

Class 73/1 front end layout showing headlight modification

Class 73/1 front end layout

Class 73/0 front end layout

All drawings supplied by Graham Fenn.

Class 73 Liveries

Above: When the first of the build emerged from Eastleigh Works it was painted in SR style coaching stock green, with small yellow warning panels on the ends, the roof was in dark grey, while the front window surrounds were in light grey, the buffer beams in red, and the underframe equipment including the bogies in black. The running numbers were applied under each cab-side window in yellow, while the carriage-style circular 'lion & wheel' emblem was applied on the bodyside. *Author's Collection*

For a comparatively small fleet the Class 73s have carried a wide and varied range of liveries. When the prototype machine No E6001 emerged from Eastleigh Carriage Works in February 1962 it was painted in SR Multiple Unit green with a small yellow warning panel. Numbering was applied under all four cab side windows in yellow. EMU-style round 'Lion and Wheel' emblems were carried in a mid-body position on each side. The remaining five locomotives of the original order Nos E6002-06 emerged in all-over green without yellow warning panels, but with the addition of a narrow grey/green band at solebar height. Numbers on these were applied in white. Underframe equipment on all six prototypes was black, air pipe fittings picked out in white, nose end electric conduit and connection boxes being finished in orange. High-visibility yellow ends were progressively applied to locomotives during the mid-1960s. By 1967 when BR's corporate identity was under development, the decision was taken that all main-line locomotives would be painted into a 'new' rail blue

scheme upon their next scheduled overhaul. This was initially with small yellow warning ends, but progressively full yellow ends were adopted as standard on grounds of added staff safety.

By 1969 the six 'JA' locomotives were in rail blue, complete with full yellow warning ends, as well as black underframes, white transfer numerals, and BR double arrow logos. This livery scheme, apart from the change of numbering to the five-digit TOPS system remained unaltered until 1984, when major changes commenced. No 73005, formerly No E6005, passed through BREL Eastleigh Works for a classified overhaul and emerged in a 'more yellow' scheme of blue body with yellow warning ends which extended round the cab sides to the rear of the cab doors, while the roof was finished in light grey and the cab window surrounds were picked out in black. Large full-height double arrow logos were applied, plus 18in high numerals. This revised livery, which surprisingly suited these locomotives, was applied to all six 'prototype' locomotives by the spring of 1987.

Right: By the time the second of the fleet emerged, a major change to the livery was made. Coaching stock green was used, but the yellow warning panels were omitted and a grey solebar added; other alterations included the repositioning of the BR emblem, the continuation of the green paint to include the cab roofs, and the picking out of the side air louvres in silver. No E6003 is seen in July 1962; note that the vacuum brake equipment and nose air pipes have yet to be fitted. *Les Elsey*

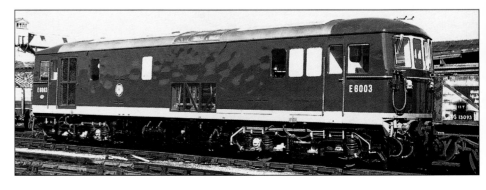

When the production fleet of Class 73/1s commenced delivery in October 1965 BR 'Electric Blue' was applied, together with small yellow warning panels, grey roof, and a solebar band of mid-grey. When delivered the first locomotive of the batch, No E6007, carried no BR emblem; however, this was soon applied at Stewarts Lane Depot. This colour scheme continued for locomotives Nos E6008-12, after when the grey solebar band was omitted. Electric Blue, a colour slightly brighter than the later BR blue, was progressively replaced by the standard shade from 1969. The last locomotive was repainted in mid-1972.

A special note must be made of No E6018, which from early 1968 operated in rail-blue livery but with wrap-around yellow ends which extended round the body sides to the rear of the cab side windows, this being part of the BRB's research in establishing the best possible warning arrangement for track staff. The locomotive was returned to conventional livery during 1969.

From the early 1970s until 1983 the Class 73 liveries remained basically unaltered with the corporate colours carried by all locomotives. The first change came in the autumn of 1983 when No 73131 received attention at BREL Eastleigh Works and emerged in the 'more yellow' colour scheme, as described previously for the Class 73/0s. This livery was authorised for the entire fleet and applied as locomotives received classified attention. A number of variations in respect of detail positions such as numbers and logo took place, especially on named examples.

Above: The illustration of No E6007 on page 24 shows that when the first of the EE locomotives emerged, no BR logo was carried; however, after the first few deliveries small double-arrow logos were applied above the resistance grilles. Locomotives Nos E6007-12 emerged with the electric-blue body, together with a grey solebar band. No E6012 is seen with TC stock at Branksome on 27 May 1967. *R. A. Panting*

Below: From No E6013 the livery was standardised on BR blue with small yellow warning panels, grey cab window surrounds and roof. This scheme is shown on No E6039 at Clapham Junction. Under the cab side window below the number, is the English Electric Vulcan Foundry works plate; this was finished in black with raised polished figures. *A. Swain*

Below: The 'as delivered' colour scheme of the Electro-Diesel fleet only remained for a short period, as by the late 1960s BR's corporate livery style was formulated, which stipulated that all main-line locomotives should be painted into the one rather drab standard scheme, this being BR blue body including roof, full yellow warning ends, black buffer beam and underframe. The four digit 'E' prefixed numbers were applied under each cab side window, and the BR logo mid-way along the body side. From 1973-74 when all locomotives were renumbered under the TOPS system, numbers were only applied under the driver's side windows. Showing the all-over rail blue, but with a non-standard grey roof and nameplate, No 73121 *Croydon 1883-1983* is seen at Stewarts Lane. *Author*

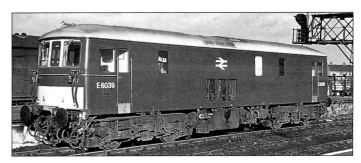

In May 1984, to mark the launch of the new 'Gatwick Express' service, locomotive No 73123, which became *Gatwick Express*, was repainted by Stewarts Lane in the then new Main Line or Executive colours of two-tone grey with a waist-height band of red and white; wrap-around yellow ends were also applied, as was an off-white roof. Half body height BR logos and large numerals occupied the upper half of the body sides. At first this striking new livery was only to be carried by No 73123; however, by late 1984 the BRB decided that this new colour scheme was acceptable as a new standard for main line passenger locomotives, and authorisation was given for all Class 73/1s to be repainted in a similar livery. The instruction came mid-way through repainting the fleet in 'more yellow' colours. As various locomotives received repaints a number of minor refinements were made to that applied to No 73123. One of the most noticeable was the continuation of the dark grey around the cab front, and the change from large-size numbers in favour of the standard size, applied under the driver's side window. The removal of the number from the upper body side permitted a revision to the nameplate position. During 1987 further Main Line livery variations came about when dark brown was applied in place of the dark-grey upper body panels for a short period. By June 1987 the final all-blue Class 73 emerged from Eastleigh BRML Workshops finished in Main Line colours.

The six 'prototype' Class 73/0 locomotives were originally deemed to retain the 'more yellow' colour scheme, as these would seldom be used on passenger workings. However, in Autumn 1987 when No 73004 was prepared for naming *The Bluebell Railway*, a 'Bluebell blue' livery similar to the later Network blue, together with wrap-around yellow ends, was applied. Subsequent shopping of 'prototype' locomotives produced some examples reverting to standard BR blue livery. The NSE all over blue was also applied to No 73005 prior to its twinning with the Mid Hants Railway.

From Spring 1988, when the new InterCity business sector was launched, it adopted its own livery, based on the previous Mainline scheme. The Class 73s started to emerge in this colour scheme, without wrap-around yellow ends, and the running number applied at first in a sub-miniature size at solebar height below the driver's-side windows. After only a relatively short period further livery modifications were made; this included the application of normal size numbers, but still in the low body position.

By the mid-1980s and the operational split-up of the railways into independent business units, several business-led identities were launched. One of the first was the application of an all-over dark grey. The first locomotive to be painted in this scheme was No 73108 at Eastleigh in 1989.

Following the formation of Network SouthEast, yet another new livery was adopted. The first Class 73 to be painted in the scheme was No 73109 prior to naming *Battle of Britain - 50th Anniversary* at Folkestone on 8 September 1990. The repaint was carried out at Selhurst and had a number of distinguishing features compared to later NSE repaints, namely the Network SouthEast legend was applied to the wide white body-side band, and sub-miniature numbers applied.

Right: The first change in livery for many years came in Autumn 1983 when No 73131 emerged from BREL Eastleigh Works in the 'more yellow' scheme; the main body, inclusive of the cab doors was finished in rail blue, but the cab ends, including the cab sides as far as the door openings were yellow. The locomotive roof was painted in a light grey, and the cab front window surrounds were picked out in black. On the sides the BR logo was almost full body height, while 18in high numbers were applied. At first, adverse criticism abounded, but in time the scheme was accepted. No 73105 displays this livery at Stewarts Lane. *Author*

Left: The big shock as far as liveries was concerned came in May 1984 when No 73123 was outshopped by Stewarts Lane in Mainline or Executive colours. BR blue was dispensed with, and the lower half of the body, including the cab doors was painted in light grey, while the top half was finished in dark grey; in the middle, dividing the two greys was a red and white band. The cab ends were painted yellow, extending as far back as the cab doors. The roof was painted light grey, and the cab window surrounds black. The number was applied mid-way along the body length on the upper grey panel in large numerals, while the logo also appeared in the upper grey band. No 73123 is seen displaying Gatwick Express livery and nameplates soon after repainting. *Author*

Above: By late 1984 Main Line colours were agreed for the Class 73/1s, repainting taking place as they passed through works, or selected for naming. The style agreed differed slightly from that applied to No 73123 in that the dark grey band was extended around the front just below cab window height, the numbers were placed under the driver's-side cab windows, and the BR logo was repositioned at the No 1 end. No 73122 *County of East Sussex* is seen at Lewes. This was the first Class 73/1 repainted into these colours by Selhurst Depot. *Author*

At the same time as the NSE livery was launched, the Civil Engineers decided to adopt a so called 'Dutch' livery in preference to the drab all-over grey. No 73133, which was undergoing a repair at Selhurst, became the first of the class to carry the colours, and emerged from the paintshop along with the first NSE variant, which provided some very interesting photographic opportunities. At the same time as its repaint the name *The Bluebell Railway* was transferred to its bodyside, as the original recipient had by then been stored. A change of ownership took No 73133 to NSE, when it saw a further livery change, being repainted to NSE colours in connection with a ceremony marking the handover of Imberhorne viaduct at East Grinstead as part of the Bluebell Railways northern extension project.

Right: Several Class 73/1s were repainted into departmental or 'general' grey during the late 1980s. No 73136 stands at Selhurst Level 4 Depot in this livery. On grey locomotives the cab window surrounds were finished in black. *Author*

Below: From the summer of 1988 revised InterCity livery was applied, consisting of the same basic scheme, but with removal of the wrap-round yellow ends, replaced by a full yellow end. The large logo was replaced by a smal- size emblem, and numbers were relegated to the base of the body side. No 73130 is shown. *Brian Morrison*

Above: Following adoption of Gatwick Express as an InterCity operation, various InterCity liveries were applied to the fleet; at first this was with the double-arrow logo on the upper side. After the introduction of InterCity branding and the swallow logo in 1987, all subsequent repaints were in this scheme. By December 1993 locomotive Nos 73201-204/206-212/235 were in the full house colours. In full InterCity colours complete with swallow logo, No 73202 *Royal Observer Corps* stands at Stewarts Lane. *Author*

A more subtle alteration in the early 1990s was the change to InterCity Swallow livery from Executive or Main Line colours for the dedicated Class 73/2 fleet used on Gatwick Express operations. The revised scheme was applied as repairs fell due at Selhurst Level 5 Depot. This livery change had one interesting side effect; the nameplates had to be repositioned to accommodate the swallow logo. When it was the turn of No 73211, it was found that

Below: To coincide with the closure of Selhurst Level 5 Depot, authority was given for the depot to repaint Class 73/0 No 73003 into near-original 1962 green livery. No E6003 stands at Selhurst just prior to its formal launch and application of a yellow end. *Author*

Above: Following introduction of business ownership of locomotives, Network SouthEast decided to paint their charges into house colours. The first Class 73/1 to be painted in Network SouthEast livery was No 73109 at Selhurst in September 1990 prior to naming *Battle of Britain 50th Anniversary*. It is seen at Selhurst, with the Network SouthEast logo painted on the white body side band, and not on the main blue body side. *Author*

Above: The most radical livery variation applied to a Class 73 was 'Pullman' colours to No 73101 in September 1991 to mark the 150th anniversary of the London-Brighton line. Repainting was carried out at Selhurst Level 5 Depot, and many of the embellishments were supplied by the VSOE company. No 73101 *Brighton Evening Argus* is seen inside Selhurst Level 5 depot. *Author*

its *County of West Sussex* plates were too long to fit between a bodyside window and grille! This locomotive was then officially de-named. The nameplates on County of East Sussex were slightly shorter and fitted into their new position with no problems which is why this locomotive (with the same number of letters as No 73211) retained its name.

In 1991 the SouthCentral sector of Network SouthEast held a number of events to celebrate the 150th anniversary of the London-Brighton line, culminating in an open day at Lovers Walk, Brighton. A train synonymous with the line is the Brighton Belle and thoughts turned to recreate the spirit of the 'Belle' by utilising the Pullman stock of the VSOE. But what would pull it? After some discussion of painting a locomotive in either Stroudley's improved engine green or Marsh umber, it was decided to apply a Pullman livery on the selected No 73101, the pioneer member of the production batch. Permission was granted by the locomotive's then sponsor, the Civil Engineers, on the condition that it would be repainted in 'Dutch' colours after the event. With assistance from Tim Robbins of VSOE, who kindly supplied paint and transfers, complemented by the customary high-quality workmanship from

Left: The Network SouthEast livery was also applied to other locomotives, with by the end of 1993 eight carrying the livery. Some slight changes were incorporated on later repaints, with the Network SouthEast legend and large size numerals being applied in white on the upper blue panel. In immaculate ex-shops condition, No 73136 *Kent Youth Music* is illustrated at Selhurst. *Author*

Selhurst Paint Shop, No 73101 duly emerged to a somewhat bewildered enthusiast world. There can be no doubt it achieved the objective of providing the icing on the cake for the Brighton celebrations; so much so that the planned repaint into 'Dutch' colours never took place, and it remained in Pullman livery until withdrawn. In parallel with this event, Selhurst Depot also repainted No 73128 in 'Dutch' livery for naming *OVS Bulleid* at Brighton.

Selhurst's reign for providing celebrity repaints came to an end in March 1993 when the Level 5 Paint and Repair Shops ceased to be an overhaul facility. To mark this occasion permission was granted to achieve a long held ambition to return one of the six Eastleigh-built locomotives to green livery. The locomotive chosen was No 73003 (E6003), which became the centre piece of the closure ceremony, when it was named *Sir Herbert Walker* in honour of the man who did so much to expand the electrification of the Southern Railway. The return of No 73003 to near-original green livery was under the control of Selhurst Level 5 Depot Manager Tony Francis. Repainting was done in two stages; during the week leading up to the naming the locomotive was repainted in all-over green as it carried when built; the nameplates were then fitted for the closure ceremony and small yellow panels applied before the locomotive took to the main line.

In May 1993 Trainload Freight SouthEast decided that the Class 73/0s were surplus to their requirements, with the exception of green liveried No 73003, which was then supported by NSE South West. Merseyrail operating services in the Liverpool area stepped in and the four remaining operational locomotives found themselves heading for a new home for the first time in 30 years. The by then 'remains' of withdrawn No 73004 followed later by road. This transfer resulted in another livery application, as Nos 73001/006 received the yellow and grey colours of MerseyRail.

Above: Prior to transfer to MerseyRail, Class 73/0 No 73006 was painted into light green livery at Stewarts Lane, which acted as a base for MerseyRail yellow to be applied at Birkenhead. The locomotive, in its unusual colours is seen at Stewarts Lane. *Darren Ford*

Above: No 73006 painted in MerseyRail yellow and grey livery, complete with MerseyRail logo and Regional Railways branding stands at Crewe in late 1994. The Class 73/0s were usually deployed on MerseyRail from Birkenhead Depot on engineers trains, as well as powering the annual 'Sandite' and de-icing trains. *Author*

Below: Following the launch of three 'shadow' freight companies in preparation for privatisation, No 73114 was repainted by Stewarts Lane into Mainline Freight aircraft blue with silver decals and numbers. With a cast Stewarts Lane depot logo under the non-driving window, No 73114 stands at Stewarts Lane Depot on 14 November 1994. *Author*

As part of the plan to privatise the railway system, Gatwick Express, which had hitherto been operated jointly with InterCity Anglia, became a self-contained business in October 1993. The livery of the Gatwick fleet subsequently underwent modification to reflect this change and the entire fleet was repainted. Although still based on the InterCity scheme, an updated image was achieved by changing the width and colour of the bodyside band from red to maroon and the application of the new 'Gatwick Express' logo.

When testing of shoegear for the Channel Tunnel Eurostar Class 373 trains was finished No 73205, which had provided power for these trains, was sent to Eastleigh for a general overhaul, and thus became the only member of the Class 73/2 fleet never to carry InterCity swallow livery. This locomotive also carried a too long nameplate - *London Chamber of Commerce* which was thus removed.

During 1994 two locomotives, Nos 73130 and 73118 were transferred to European Passenger Services (EPS) to assist transfer of Eurostar stock when it could not operate under its own power, or to shunt stock at North Pole Depot. For this role both locomotives were modified with Scharfenberg couplings and repainted in two-tone Railfreight style grey-livery with Channel Tunnel side branding.

In November 1994 Trainload Freight South East was relaunched as Mainline Freight as a shadow private operator in preparation for full privatisation. To coincide with this event No 73114 was repainted into the new house colours of aircraft blue with silver logos. Repainting was carried out at Stewarts Lane. At the same time the locomotive was named *Stewarts Lane Traction Maintenance Depot*.

The rapid privatisation of the UK rail system saw only a handful of Class 73s repainted into Mainline Freight blue, before the scheme

Above: The first Class 73 to carry EW&S livery, No 73128 stands outside Stewarts Lane electric shed on 20 August 1996. At this time the '&' was still incorporated in the company bodyside logo and the 'animal head' motif was yet to be devised. This locomotive carries a 73A Stewarts Lane depot plate on the front end and has its buck-eye coupling in the raised position. *Author*

Left: The two Class 73/1s, Nos 73118 and 73130 taken over by European Passenger Services and modified at Crewe Works with hinged Scharfenberg couplings were painted in railfreight-style 'triple grey' colours, offset by the three 'Channel Tunnel segment' logos on the bodyside. No 73118, with No 73130 in the rear poses at North Pole Depot in June 2004. *Author*

was placed on hold with the announcement of the sale of all three shadow privatised freight companies to the American-based subsidiary of the Wisconsin Central Railroad, who in the UK traded as English Welsh & Scottish (EWS) Railway.

By August 1996 the first Class 73/1 had been refurbished by Stewarts Lane depot and No 73128 was rolled out on 20 August sporting maroon and gold corporate colours with the EW&S logo on the side. The scheme was principally all-over maroon off-set by a deep gold band running cab to cab onto which the logo and number were applied. The maroon extended over the roof and around the upper section of the cab end. High visibility yellow was applied to the lower front end. By mid-October a second ED, No 73131 emerged in the livery.

As time came to prove changes in EWS traction policy saw the Class 73s phased out and there were only ever two examples painted in EWS maroon.

A minor livery variation appeared in November 1996 when the South West Trains Class 73/1 'Thunderbird' No 73109 emerged with the legend 'A Stagecoach Company' on the bodyside.

By 2001 with the Gatwick Express operation investing in new rolling stock, some of the Class 73/2 fleet became surplus to requirements. The then infrastructure operator Railtrack purchased two locomotives, Nos 73212 and 73213, which they passed through private engineering company Fragonset Railways in Derby for an overhaul and repaint. The pair emerged in June carrying Railtrack blue and green with a large Railtrack legend on the body side. This livery remained until autumn 2005 when Fragonset Railways, now trading as FM Rail, repainted the pair in Network Rail yellow livery.

Another beneficiary of the replacement of Gatwick Express locomotive-hauled operations with multiple-unit technology was GB Railways - now part of FirstGroup. The company purchased six of the redundant Class 73/2s from owner Porterbrook Leasing and

Below: South West Trains retained one Class 73 (No 73109) under privatisation to act as a 'Thunderbird' locomotive. This retained the basic Network SouthEast colour scheme with orange replacing the red bodyside band until 2005 when a full South West Trains 'Desiro' style colour scheme was adopted, being applied to No 73109 by East Wimbledon Depot. When SWT obtained two further 'Thunderbirds,' Nos 73201 and 73235, these were also repainted into the distinctive livery. No 73109 is shown below left in the late 1990s Stagecoach-SWT colours, while below right No 73235 shows the 2005-applied SWT Desiro scheme. *Darren Ford/Brian Morrison*

originally stored the locomotives before returning them to front line traffic for engineering train operation. The restoration work carried out by Fragonset in Derby saw a very distinctive blue, orange and yellow livery applied. An operational fleet of four locomotives entered service in July 2004.

Fragonset Railways, now FM Rail, purchased a handful of Class 73s offered for disposal. The Company rebuilt No 73107 and returned it to the main line as a spot hire locomotive in autumn 2004,

painted in the company's black livery offset by deep red bodyside branding and a cast company logo.

South West Trains, who have operated a Class 73 since privatisation, increased its fleet from one to three locomotives from mid-2005 to provide enhanced 'Thunderbird' capability for the Desiro EMU fleet. All three of the South West Trains Class 73s are now painted in the latest blue-swirl Desiro livery applied at East Wimbledon depot.

Left: Following redundancy by Gatwick Express, the Class 73/2s were returned to owner Porterbrook Leasing who sought new operators. UK rail infrastructure owner Railtrack took on a pair, Nos 73212 and 73213 and sent them to Fragonset Railways in Derby for overhaul. Repainting saw the pair display the blue and green 'arc' livery of the company, supplemented by the Railtrack legend on the bodyside. No 73212 is illustrated. *Darren Ford*

Below: After the demise of Railtrack and the formation of Network Rail, the two Class 73s passed to Network Rail. After seeing a long period out of traffic, the duo were fitted with OTMR equipment in mid-2005 and repainted by FM Rail Derby into the latest Network Rail all-over yellow livery, shown here on No 73121 at Tonbridge. In 2005/06 the pair are frequently used by GBRf. *Pat Seale*

Right: Derby-based Fragonset Railways purchased a number of Class 73s offered for disposal. A number are stored around the UK at various heritage sites, while one, No 73107, has been returned to full mainline operation. In late 2004 the locomotive was repainted in Fragonset black livery, shown here at Faversham soon after being named *Spitfire.*
Kendal May

Below: The most striking of the recent ED liveries is the deep blue, orange and yellow of GB Railfreight (GBRf), a part of FirstGroup. At the end of 2005, the company owned eight Class 73s, although only four were in the corporate livery scheme. In common with several recent ED overhauls and repaints, the work was undertaken at the Derby facility of Fragonset Railways. No 73209 is illustrated at York.
Ron Cover

Class 73 Driving cabs

T he Class 73 locomotives were fitted with dual-position driving controls, enabling driving and the operation of most auxiliaries to take place from both sides of the cab, this facility was stipulated during the design stage on the grounds of safety for yard and depot working. Although this dual-position cab layout was accepted on the SR, and indeed fitted into the Region's Type 3 (Class 33) diesel locomotives, no other locomotives except for shunting machines have this very useful attribute.

With the Class 73s being dual-powered locomotives, operational under both electric and diesel conditions, the cab layout is somewhat unorthodox, in having two power controllers at each driving position. However only one is, and can be, used at the same time. The upper handle, with a round grip, is used for electric operation, while the lower handle, which has a square grip, is used for diesel or auxiliary power operation. The electric controller features hand notch-up, or automatic 'run-up' positions, while the diesel controller is of the standard progressive type, giving a varied power output dependent on its position. To the side of the power controllers is the driver's key socket and master switch, used for selection of direction.

On the left side of the driving position are two brake controllers; the one on the far left, slightly recessed into the body wall, is a straight air brake valve, which operates the brakes on the locomotive only, the slightly larger valve to the front is an automatic air/vacuum/ep brake controller which operates train brakes, as well as those on the locomotive, in a progressive movement as the brake handle is moved in an anti-clockwise direction. On the cab wall above the straight air brake valve is a 'Loudaphone', providing buzzer and speech communication between the driver and guard of a suitably fitted train. An Automatic Warning System (AWS) 'sunflower' indicator is fitted above the automatic brake valve. AWS equipment was not fitted to the Class 73s until the 1980s, to conform to modern safety requirements, in common with Slow Speed Fitment (SSF), which vents the brake pipe if the master switch is moved above 7mph. More recently Train Protection Warning System (TPWS) has been fitted.

Other desk equipment is basically standard, with items identified on the illustration. Although the original prototype and later production locomotives have basically the same cab, some variations on equipment style will be found.

Above: Class 73/1 cab layout, driver's side: 1 - Loudaphone, 2 - Straight air brake valve, 3 - Automatic brake valve (air/vacuum/ep), 4 - AWS 'sunflower' indicator, 5 - Sand apply button, 6 - Exhauster speed-up button, 7 - Brake selector switch (automatic air/ep), 8 - Anti-slip brake button, 9 - Rear horn button, 10 - AWS reset button, 11 - Driver's windscreen wiper valve, 12 - Horn valve, 13 - Shoes down button, 14 - Main reservoir and train pipe pressure gauge, 15 - Brake cylinder pressure gauge, 16 - Vacuum gauge, 17 - Control resistance flag, 18 - Line supply flag, 19 - Engine running flag, 20 - Auxiliary power flag, 21 - Wheelslip flag, 22 - Fault flag, 23 - Speedometer, 24 - Traction ammeter, 25 - Driver's window demister switch, 26 - Route indicator light switch, 27 - Driver's instrument light switch, 28 - Engine stop switch, 29 - Auto engine start switch, 30 - Auxiliary power off switch, 31 - Auxiliary power on switch, 32 - Overload reset switch, 33 - Fire alarm test switch, 34 - Electric power controller, 35 - Diesel power controller, 36 - Master switch, 37 - Driver's key socket.

Right: Driver's assistant's side cab layout Class 73/0. 1 - Train heat 'off' switch, 2 - Train heat 'on' switch, 3 - Interlock cut-out switch (used for single pole train heating later removed), 4 - Driver's side cab heat, 5 - Driver's assistant's side cab heat, 6 - Electric power controller, 7 - Diesel power controller, 8 - Master switch, 9 - Fire alarm test switch, 10 - Horn valve, 11 - Anti-slip brake button, 12 - Driver's assistant's windscreen wiper valve, 13 - Shoe down button, 14 - Automatic brake valve, 15 - Straight air brake valve, 16 - Exhauster speed-up button, 17 - Sand apply button. *Author*

Above: Class 73/0 cab layout, showing clearly the twin driving positions. If this and the illustration opposite are compared a number of minor detail differences will be apparent. The cab illustrated is of No E6001 when new. *Author*

Left: Class 73/1 power controller. The top electric controller has the following functions: 'Lock Off'- the controller is shut down. 'Off' - used to shut off power. 'Run Back' - controller is placed here when the driver requires to reduce the locomotive's power output. 'Hold' - used to hold the camshaft power position. 'Notch-up' - used to take power in progressive stages. The driver moves the controller between the 'hold' and 'notch-up' positions; for each movement between these points power is increased. 'Run-up (ser)' - to obtain this the driver has to depress a button in the end of the controller; when in run-up (ser) the locomotive will automatically increase power to full series. 'Run-up (par)' - this position is obtained in a similar way to 'Run-up (ser)', but takes the electrics to full parallel position. 'Run-up (WF)' - this position, again obtained by depressing the power controller end button, automatically takes the locomotive's traction motors to a full weak field position. The lower controller, used for diesel operation has three marked positions 'Lock Off' which is where the controller is kept when not in use, 'Off' which shuts off the generator output from the traction motors, and power. When the driver requires power he moves the controller to any position between the off and full power position, obtaining a variable output to the traction motors. *Author*

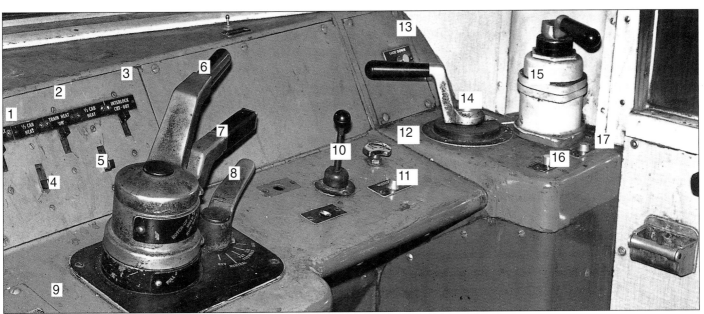

The Game of the Name

After many years when the Railway Executive decided that naming of its motive power was not to be encouraged, a complete turn-round of policy came in the late 1970s. Firstly complete fleets or classes were deemed 'to be named' - such as the Class 50s and 87s. Soon regional and in some cases depot representations were made regarding further naming of members of virtually all classes.

Following the use of Class 73 No 73142 to haul the empty stock for the Mountbatten funeral train between Clapham Junction and Waterloo on 5 September 1979, and the use of Class 33s Nos 33027/056 to haul the funeral train to Romsey, considerable pressure was placed on the Southern Region, and the British Railways Board to name the locomotives in association with the late Earl. By early 1980 the BRB gave approval to name all three machines, the two Class 33s becoming *Earl Mountbatten of Burma* and *The Burma Star*, while the Class 73 was allocated the name *Broadlands*, after the Mountbatten ancestral home in Romsey.

The day set for naming of the first Class 73, No 73142 (now 73201) was 25 August 1980. Of course the locomotive's home depot, Stewarts Lane, was given the task of preparation. Depot Engineer Keith Parsons took charge of the operation, while 'on the day' arrangements at Romsey were looked after by the Regional Public Relations Officer. No 73142, which for some time had been a favourite of Stewarts Lane, was taken out of service on 1 August and placed in the Electric shed short road, where a complete repaint was carried out to the highest standard. By the end of the first week of August the two corporate-style cast nameplates had arrived from the foundry at BREL Swindon Works, and the four Heraldic shields from a private supplier. The nameplates and shields were offered up for the first time on 23 August and affixed during the afternoon by the depot carriage and wagon staff. After official photographs were taken the plates and shields were covered in plywood sheets in readiness for the locomotive's transfer to Romsey. During the afternoon of 24 August the locomotive was given a service check and placed 'on-charge' to ensure no problems the following day.

After the naming was agreed it was decided to invite Lord Romsey to unveil the nameplates, a task which he readily agreed to perform. Several weeks prior to the ceremony, when crewing arrangements were under discussion, it was agreed that the same men who operated the locomotive into Waterloo on the day of the funeral train would be rostered for the naming duty. So all was set for the big day. Soon after 06.00 on 25 August depot staff made a final inspection of No 73142 and found all in order; just prior to 09.00 Waterloo-based Driver Maurice Boyce and Driver's Assistant Paul Stoneman, together with Regional Motive Power Inspector

Below: The actual unveiling of the nameplates on No 73142, now No 73201, was carried out by Lord Romsey at Romsey station on 25 September 1980, at the invitation of the then SR General Manager John Pallett. Lord Romsey is seen unveiling the plate with John Pallett looking on. *Author*

Cyril Stevens, arrived to collect the locomotive. No 73142 operated light to Romsey via Woking, Basingstoke, and Eastleigh arriving at Romsey via the then freight-only line from Eastleigh. While a number of special arrangements had been made at Romsey, the actual naming had to fit in with the scheduled passenger/freight services; this dictated that No 73142 could occupy the platform for just 25 minutes. Lord Romsey, at the invitation of SR General Manager John Pallett, unveiled the plates under the watchful eye of the Countess Mountbatten of Burma. After the ceremony and departure of guests for refreshments at Broadlands House, No 73142, bearing its resplendent Broadlands nameplates, worked back to Stewarts Lane to take up normal duties. From that day No 73142 was the flagship of the fleet, operating virtually all SR Royal Trains, before becoming part of the Gatwick Express fleet and now operated by South West Trains.

The second Class 73 naming was first mooted in the summer of 1980, with a ceremony set for 3 December this time. The name chosen was *Brighton Evening Argus*, to be applied to No 73101 to mark the newspaper's 100th anniversary. Again Stewarts Lane was given the preparation task, with the locomotive being removed from traffic during mid-November for repainting and preparation work. As the naming was to celebrate the centenary of the newspaper it was agreed to renumber the locomotive to 73100 for the event, an identity which the locomotive retained for the remainder of December. No 73100 was completed only hours prior to the naming, and operated light to Brighton on the morning of the event. The actual unveiling was carried out by Mrs D Williams, the wife of the newspaper's editor, under the watchful eyes of civic and railway guests. After No 73100 was christened it made a number of light runs up and down the platform, conveying newspaper and civic guests on the footplate.

After these first two high-profile naming events a number of other locomotives received cast plates. Some of the more interesting events are detailed.

A major highlight in Class 73 history came in May 1984, to coincide with the launch of the 'Gatwick Express' 15min interval service linking London Victoria with Gatwick Airport. The 'new' service was to be operated by rebuilt Mk2 locomotive-hauled stock with Class 73s at one end and a Gatwick luggage van (rebuilt from Class 414 EMU stock) at the other. To promote the service, the latest Executive livery of two-tone grey with a white and red waist band was applied to the passenger stock. Early in 1980, long before the service was inaugurated, agreement was reached to name a Class 73 *Gatwick Express*, as an added promotion to the service launch. The locomotive selected was No 73123. Agreement was then sought to repaint it into the then-new Executive colours, matching the stock. This was granted, and during April the locomotive was taken out of service for preparation at Stewarts Lane. Apart from a thorough technical overhaul, the largest job was the repainting; for this the locomotive was placed in the redundant carriage and wagon shop, adjacent to the electric shed, where it was handed over to the depot painter. By the first week of May most body work was completed, and an attempt was then made to keep viewers at bay as the livery change was supposed to be secret until its official launch. To prove to the M&EE that the locomotive was in good technical condition, and suitable for its special charge, it operated a high-speed test between Stewarts Lane and Brighton during the week prior to its naming, under the cover of darkness. The BREL Swindon-produced nameplates were fitted on 8 May under the supervision of Depot Engineer Keith Parsons, and other M&EE department representatives. The official naming was carried out on 10 May, a few days prior to the introduction of the new service by Councillor Mrs P Sitwell, Mayor of Westminster, at Victoria Station.

Above: As mentioned in the text, Stewarts Lane was responsible for the final preparation of most Class 73s prior to naming; this work included fitting of the cast nameplates, and shields. Usually after names were applied, which was often several days prior to actual unveiling ceremonies, plywood covers were fitted, ensuring that no photographs were taken prior to the official event. *Broadlands* is seen having covers fitted over its plates at Stewarts Lane on 24 September 1980. *Author*

Above: No 73142 *Broadlands* was the first Class 73 to be named, which soon became the flagship of the fleet. Under the Broadlands name were two heraldic shields, on the left that of Test Valley, and on the right, the Borough of Romsey. *Author*

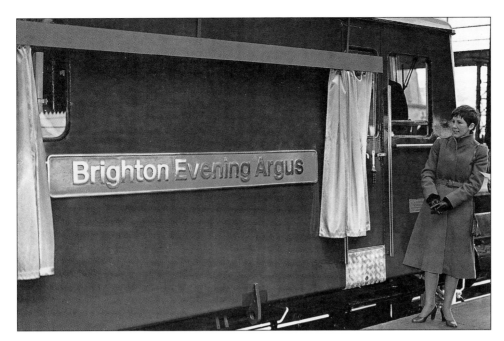

Left: The ceremony to unveil the nameplates on No 73101 (73100) was carried out by the newspaper editor's wife Mrs D Williams, who is seen looking at the plate just seconds after pulling the cord at Brighton station on 3 December 1980. *Author*

Probably the greatest honour that could ever be granted to Stewarts Lane Depot was permission to name one of their EDs after the depot. When the suggestion was first put forward it was the intention to name the pioneer member of the fleet, No 73001, and at the same time repaint the locomotive into original green livery - however at the time the BRB ruled that repainting into green would not be permitted. This was followed by an amount of disagreement between the operating departments as to whether the passenger business wanted a locomotive named Stewarts Lane - although it was this depot's expert skills that were responsible for the reliability of the Gatwick Express operation, which had become very profitable. Differences of opinion were smoothed out in the summer of 1985, and it was agreed to name aptly numbered 73125 *Stewarts Lane 1860-1985* at the Depot's Open Day on 22 September marking 125 years of railway activity at this London site. Some three and a half weeks prior to naming, No 73125 was removed from service - and needless to say repainted into Executive colours to the very highest of standards. The BREL Swindon cast nameplates were fitted under the supervision of M&EE representative Les Chatfield on 20 September. It is worthy of note that these plates were some of the last to be cast at the Swindon

foundry, and their poor quality reflected the imminent demise of this site. Repainting and preparation of No 73125 ran a little behind schedule, and on the morning of the open day the numbers and other details were still being applied when the first depot visitors arrived. The honour of unveiling the Stewarts Lane name fell to two of the longest serving staff at the depot, Mr J Head, and Mr H Loader, who were invited to christen 'their' locomotive by the then Southern General Manager Gordon Pettit, under the watchful eye of the Mayor of Lambeth.

Another naming close to the hearts of many railway staff came on 19 October 1985 when No 73134 was named *Woking Homes 1885-1985*. This locomotive was painted in full Executive livery as part of a classified overhaul at BREL Eastleigh Works; however, Stewarts Lane took the locomotive out of service two weeks prior to the naming for cleaning and nameplate fixing. Many people were surprised by the choice of location and person selected to unveil the plates on No 73134, when Mrs P Bohling, Mayor of Woking was given the task at Waterloo Station, in preference to a resident of the home or staff member at Woking. After the ceremony No 73134 worked a special to Woking carrying some of the Homes' residents.

Right: No 73121, later 73208 *Croydon 1883 - 1983* was the first ED to carry a double line plate, below which is the Borough coat of arms. *Author*

Below: No 73102 (73212) was one of the few locomotives named after a non-UK company carrying the name of Swiss-based air tour operator *Airtour Suisse.* Below the plate was the red/white Airtour Suisse logo. *Author*

Right: One of the proudest days for Stewarts Lane Depot was on 22 September 1985, when No 73125 was named *Stewarts Lane 1860-1985*; the unveiling was officiated by two of Stewarts Lane's longest serving staff, Mr J Head and Mr H Loader. The two unveilers, with Mr Head on the left are seen pulling the cord under the watchful eye of SR General Manager Gordon Pettit, the Mayor of Lambeth and SR Press officer Dick Marks. *Author*

Selhurst depot had long been associated with the Class 73 fleet and in autumn 1986 the depot was honoured for its association by a naming. No 73116 was named *Selhurst*, this being performed at the depot during a staff open day to mark the completion and full opening of the new EMU/locomotive Level 4 inspection facility. After the nameplates were unveiled No 73116 was driven through an opening banner across the depot doors.

No 73118 was named *The Romney Hythe and Dymchurch Railway* in a ceremony at Folkestone Harbour station on 8 May 1987. The decision to name a BR locomotive after this 'light' railway was agreed, as the event marked the 60th anniversary of the RH&DR; plate unveiling was carried out by BBC commentator Brian Johnston OBE. Other dignitaries attending the ceremony included BRs local Manager Cedric Nott and the Managing Director of the RH&DR, John Snell. The nameplate fitted to No 73118 was, at the time, the largest on any BR locomotive, and also carried a RH&DR coat of arms below.

The first of the six prototype locomotives to carry a name was No 73004 named *The Bluebell Railway* after the successful Sussex-based light railway. Unveiling of the specially-prepared locomotive,

repainted in 'Bluebell blue' by Stewarts Lane, was carried out at East Grinstead station by Johnny Morris, Vice President of the Bluebell Railway Preservation Society on 19 September 1987.

On 16 May 1988 it was the turn of the Travelling Post Office (TPO) to be honoured when, to mark the introduction of revised Travelling Post Office services, including the introduction of a new TPO to/from Dover, as well as marking the 150th anniversary of the service, No 73138 was named *Post Haste – 150 Years of Travelling Post Offices* in a ceremony at Tonbridge. It held the distinction of being the first named locomotive painted in the 'new' InterCity livery.

A further light railway was twinned with BR in September 1988 when 'JA' No 73005 was named *Mid Hants - Watercress Line* in a ceremony at Waterloo Station, after which the locomotive hauled a train to Alton and the Mid Hants Railway.

In September 1990 a name change took place, when the name *The Bluebell Railway* applied to 73/0 No 73004 was removed, to be re-applied to Class 73/1 No 73133 without ceremony at Selhurst Level 5 Depot. The locomotive was the first to be painted in 'Dutch' (yellow/grey) livery, unveiled at Selhurst on 6 September, which

Right: After *Airtour Suisse* was named at Gatwick Airport a bottle of champagne was broken over the buffer. This was the first time this tradition, practised for many years in nautical circles, was carried out at a locomotive naming ceremony. Fräulein Katarin Rentsch is seen cutting the champagne bottle release wire and the bottle smashing over the buffer. *Author*

Ashford, from where it was moved by road to the K&ESR. At the time, this was the first occasion that an operational BR locomotive had visited a private line which was not rail connected. The naming event was held at Northiam Station and was carried out jointly by Councillor Harry Hatcher, Chairman of East Sussex Council and Councillor John Perry, Vice-Chairman of Kent County Council. The event of having the BR locomotive operating on the private line was also used to launch the line's Robertsbridge extension project. No 73126 operated on the K&ESR until 29 May when it was returned by road to Sevington to be reunited with the BR network.

A Class 73 renaming took place in May 1992, when the by then Pullman-liveried No 73101 had its *Brighton Evening Argus* plates removed by Stewarts Lane and the name *The Royal Alex'* applied. This is the name of the children's hospital in Brighton, which was supported by many fundraising events in the area. It was agreed that while a special 'Rocking Horse' appeal for equipment was continuing, the names would be applied to the locomotive. It was announced at the naming that at the end of the appeal the plates will be removed and raffled, with the proceeds going to the appeal. The original names would then be reapplied, but with changes to the rail industry this was never done. The locomotive was not repainted for the 1992 ceremony, but touched up by Stewarts Lane Depot. Unveiling of the plates was carried out by a young patient of the hospital in a ceremony at Brighton Station.

One of the more interesting Class 73 namings took place on 31 March 1993, when the name *Sir Herbert Walker*, after the first General Manager of the Southern Railway, was applied to Class 73/0 No 73003. The locomotive was repainted in original green livery for the event, which sadly marked the closure of Selhurst Level 5 Depot. Over the previous years this site had been responsible for numerous overhauls and repaints of this class. Repainting of the locomotive was carried out during March, with

conveniently marked the 30th anniversary of the historic Sussex light railway.

The Selhurst Level 5 Depot gradually became responsible for the repainting of locomotives prior to special events during the early 1990s. One of the most significant was the repainting of No 73109 into full Network SouthEast colours during late August in preparation for naming *Battle of Britain – 50th Anniversary*. The locomotive was given a complete technical and cosmetic overhaul at Selhurst, emerging on 6 September for a special photo-call in the Depot yard, for which Depot Manager Tony Francis had arranged to park the newly-named *The Bluebell Railway* alongside. The naming of No 73109 was carried out at Folkestone Central Station as part of the Battle of Britain 50th anniversary celebrations, by Lord Ilchester, President of the Royal Air Force Association (south) on 8 September. The naming event also coincided with the running of 4-6-2 'Battle of Britain' No 34072 *257 Squadron* in the Folkestone-Dover area.

On 23 May 1991 a very unusual naming took place, when No 73126 was named *Kent & East Sussex Light Railway*. For this event the locomotive was outshopped in the latest NSE livery by Selhurst Level 5 Depot, and then moved by rail to Sevington near

Right: One of the naming highlights of 1991 was on 23 May when Network SouthEast agreed to the naming of No 73126 as *Kent & East Sussex Railway*. For the event the locomotive was repainted into NSE colours and transported to the K&ES Railway for a week's special operation. This was the first time an operational BR locomotive had been taken to a land-locked rail centre for loan. Standing by the immense nameplate are Admiral Sir Linsay Bryson, Councillor John Perry, NSE Director Geoff Harrison Mee and Councillor Harry Hatcher. *Author*

a special roll-out without nameplates and yellow warning ends on 27 March. The naming ceremony was held inside the Level 5 Depot on 31 March, when the plates were unveiled by ITV newscaster Nick Owen, who was a founder member of the Southern Electric Group and a life-long railway enthusiast.

Another naming of interest took place on 3 June when No 73109 *Battle of Britain – 50th Anniversary* was renamed *Force 'O' Weymouth* as part of the 50th anniversary celebrations for D-Day. Force 'O' was an American landing force which set off from Weymouth for the D-Day landings in France. The interest in this naming was that the original Battle of Britain plates were left applied, but covered with wood. The Force 'O' Weymouth name was carried for just one month, after which the original name was uncovered once again.

To mark the official launch of the new Mainline Freight Company on 14 November 1994, No 73114 was repainted into the new house colours at Stewarts Lane Depot. During the course of the launch event the locomotive was bestowed with the nameplate *Stewarts Lane Traction Maintenance Depot*; unveiling of the plate was carried out by Stewarts Lane Mainline Freight Depot Engineer Graham Preston and Mainline Freight Engineering Director Brian Harris. The plates were finished with a silver/grey background with letters picked out in blue.

After the naming events of 1994 it was a staggering 10 years before any further Class 73s were named. However during that period a number of de-namings took place reflecting ownership change and privatisation.

In September 2004 private operator Fragonset Railways returned locomotive No 73107 to frontline use, repainting it into company black livery. To mark its return to traffic it was named *Spitfire* in association with Kent brewer Shepherd Neame. Unveiling was

One of the most significant events in Class 73 history was on 23 May 1991 when Network SouthEast agreed to the naming of No 73126 *Kent & East Sussex Railway*. For the event the locomotive was repainted into NSE colours and moved to the K&ES Railway for a week's special operation. No 73126 is seen at Tenterden Town Station with a train bound for Northiam. *Author*

carried out at Faversham Station on 5 September, the cast plate being supplemented by a cast Spitfire aircraft logo above and a cast Spitfire label as applied to the Shepherd Neame real ale of the same name.

To mark the entry into traffic of GB Railfreight's four Class 73s, a multiple naming ceremony took place at Victoria Station on 12 October 2004 when each of the Company's locomotives was named after a female member of GBRf staff. Each locomotive was unveiled by the 'owning' lady: 73204 *Janice* by Janice Baptiste, the PA to the GBRf Operations Director; 73205 *Jeanette* by Jeanette Smith, the GBRf Office Manager; 73206 *Lisa* by Lisa Lane, GBRf Strategic Planning Manager, and 73209 *Alison* by Alison Irving, GBRf Yard Manager at Whitemoor. The nameplate style adopted was of the traditional design.

A naming event close to the hearts of many South London railwaymen took place at Stewarts Lane Gatwick Express Depot on 22 July 2005 when the last operational Gatwick Express Class 73/2, No 73202 was named *Dave Berry* after the longest-serving member of Gatwick Express staff and the most senior Class 73 engineer frequently known as 'Doctor ED'. Dave had worked at Stewarts Lane with the fleet for more than 40 years. The naming officially marked the final locomotive-hauled Gatwick Express service. No 73202 does, however, remain with Gatwick Express for 'Thunderbird' duties.

Class 73/1 No 73136 (E6043), privately owned by a consortium of seven and saved from the breakers yard at Booths, Rotherham, has been returned to main-line condition and painted in 1960s style blue, and in late 2005 was hired to GBRf. To mark the remarkable achievement of returning this locomotive to operation it was named *Perseverance* in July 2005 by its owners at Stewarts Lane.

Above: Graham Preston (left), Stewarts Lane Depot Engineer, and Brian Harris (right), Engineering Director of Mainline Freight, stand by the nameplate of No 73114 *Stewarts Lane Traction Maintenance Depot* on 14 November 1994 immediately after unveiling. *Author*

Below: There are few serving railwaymen in the UK who have had their name applied to a locomotive, one exception in 'Doctor ED' - Dave Berry who has been associated with the maintenance of the class for over 40 years. Dave stands by 'his' plate on No 73202 in July 2005. *Author*

Below: When GB Railfreight launched their fleet of Class 73s in autumn 2004, the batch of four were all named after GBRf female staff members. Lisa Lane, GBRf Strategic Planning Manager stands by 'her' Class 73 at Victoria just after naming. *Darren Ford*

Above: Named ED No 73142 *Broadlands* broke new ground for a class member on 24 April 1982 when, in multiple with Class 33 No 33027 *Earl Mountbatten of Burma*, it worked light from Stewarts Lane Depot to Laira Depot to take part in an open day event the following day. Arrangements between the photographer and the SR control were made, enabling the ED to trail between Salisbury and Exeter from where it led along the sea wall section via Dawlish, Teignmouth and Newton Abbot to Plymouth. The pair are seen emerging from Parsons Tunnel, Teignmouth. *Author*

The Gatwick Express

Above: During the weeks leading up to the introduction of the Gatwick Express service, the stock was amassed at Stewarts Lane depot - the base for the new operation. Resplendent in its new colours, No 73123 *Gatwick Express* stands coupled to 'GE' stock in the depot yard. *Author*

The Gatwick Express trains we saw for more than 20 years powered by Class 73/2s would never have been, but for the general growth in aviation which occurred during the late 1920s and early 1930s. This eventually led to the purchase of Lowfield Heath and surrounding Surrey farmland in March 1930, and the granting of a private aerodrome licence a few months later, which paved the way for Gatwick Airport and its adjoining station, and this led to the 1980s Gatwick Express service.

In 1933 the Southern Railway commissioned an outside business to produce a report on how the railway could participate in projected aviation development. Their suggestions included the creation of integrated rail-air services to the continent, Isle of Wight and Channel Islands for which the proposed new Airport at Gatwick afforded many advantages. This was at the time, developed by a private firm, Airports Ltd, which numbered among its directors Sir Felix Pole, the former General Manager of the GWR. To feed this new air facility the SR was to provide a station at Tinsley Green, helped by a financial contribution and a revenue guarantee from Airports Ltd.

The 'new' station was one mile south of the existing Gatwick Racecourse station, and opened for local traffic on 30 September 1935. Flights from the airport commenced in May 1936 and the station was renamed Gatwick Airport from 1 June the same year. When it opened the station was served by three trains per hour in each direction, including the Victoria-Brighton semi-fast services, and at that time was ample to cover the passenger loadings. Despite problems, including lack of terminal facilities, the airport attracted a growing traffic level to France, the Channel Islands, and

later the Isle of Wight. With the outbreak of hostilities in September 1939, civil aviation in Southern England was drastically curtailed and Gatwick Airport was requisitioned by the RAF. Considerable alterations to the rail service were also made during the war years.

When war ended in 1945 civilian flying resumed from Gatwick but with the nationalisation of UK air transport, scheduled services were concentrated on London's new airport at Heathrow. This was still far from complete when in 1953 the need for a second airport near to London was recognised, and the choice of the small grass airfield at Gatwick for expansion into a major international airport was made. The Ministry of Civil Aviation acquired the racecourse to the north of the existing airfield in 1953 to provide the site for a larger runway and terminal buildings for the new Airport. British Railways also erected new station buildings on the old racecourse platforms and linked them by a footbridge to the new airport terminal. Airport and station came into use on 27 May 1958, and at the same time the old Gatwick Airport station was closed.

From opening of the new station the existing three trains per hour to London were supplemented by extending the half-hourly stopping trains from Horsham on the Mid-Sussex line from Three Bridges to Victoria, and attaching a portion for air travellers at Gatwick.

During the late 1950s and early 1960s a considerable number of airline charter companies established their London operations at Gatwick and by the end of 1960 the annual passenger turnover for the airport had reached 470,000, with a significant number of these travellers using the adjoining station for travel to and from the airport. At this time most passengers travelled on the half-hourly

Above: For several weeks prior to the commencement of public operation, test and trial GE formations were operated. In conjunction with brake testing, Class 73/1 No 73132 was seconded to the development section at Strawberry Hill and operated with a five-car Gatwick set plus GLV No 9105 on numerous specials between Strawberry Hill, Woking, and Basingstoke. One of the test specials is seen arriving at Basingstoke on 24 April 1984. *Author*

fast services to London, but if a flight was diverted to Gatwick, or an exceptional number of passengers was foreseen, special trains had to be arranged. With the increased traffic mainly from the growing charter business, BR decided to introduce a night train service from May 1967. Passenger returns on these services were not excessive but sufficient enough for them to be retained in a period when uneconomic trains were likely to be axed. During the mid-1960s and early 1970s the airports and in turn, the railway passenger figures gradually increased, mainly due to scheduled flights starting to use the airport, and larger aircraft being introduced. By the end of 1966 the yearly turnover for airport passengers had reached the one million mark. The increase in air

travel continued, and by 1978, 99% of the London-based charter operations were using Gatwick. This potentially vast number of passengers, which could yet increase, called for still further alterations to the rail services and in May 1978 BR introduced the 'Rapid City-Link' 15 minute-interval service. For this duty, trains were formed of converted 4VEP EMUs, which had 24 seats per unit removed and luggage racks fitted; the specially adapted units were reclassified 4VEG (4car Vestibule Electro Gatwick). Although BR had a fleet of 12 VEG units, Nos 7901-7912, it was not always possible to keep the units solely on the London-Gatwick run.

Other rail alterations were carried out in 1978, which included changes to the track layout at Gatwick to improve train turnaround

Right: Seven train sets were originally required to operate the 15 minute interval Gatwick Express service, and to assist in train identification target numbers were carried for the first few months of operation. No 73123 *Gatwick Express* on train No 2 heads the 09.15 Victoria-Gatwick Airport near Streatham North Junction on 18 April 1985. *Author*

arrangements. A start was also made on the total rebuilding of Gatwick Airport Station, a major undertaking which took some four years to complete.

In 1981 BR announced that in conjunction with its Brighton line modernisation scheme and continued growth at Gatwick Airport, a new 'Gatwick Express' service would be introduced, dedicated entirely to London-Gatwick passengers. The one major factor to be determined was the stock to be utilised; although the railways had considerable investment for the virtual rebuilding of the Brighton line the budget would not cover the building of new trains; however, finance could be found for the complete rebuilding of some existing locomotive-hauled coaches, and the special adaptation of driving cars from redundant EMUs.

The passenger stock for Gatwick Express services was converted from locomotive-hauled MkIIf coaches accommodating 41 in first class and 56 in standard class vehicles, special luggage racks being provided at coach ends and between seat backs. For their new role, the cars were also technically modified for SR-style multiple unit control. Three different passenger vehicle types were introduced - TS (Trailer Standard), TSH (Trailer Standard Handbrake) and TFH (Trailer First Handbrake). For operational ease the cars were semi-permanently coupled into two and three-coach sets: two-coach sets classified 488/2 are formed TSH, TFH, and three-car sets classified 488/3 are formed TSH, TS, TSH. Within each set the conventional drawgear and buck-eye couplers were removed in favour of solid shank couplings, while at set ends buck-eye couplings were retained, but high level control jumpers and air connections fitted, enabling compatibility with 1951, 57, 63, and 66 stock as well as push-pull fitted locomotives.

During 1991-92 a major refurbishment programme was undertaken by BREL Ltd (ABB) at Derby Litchurch Lane, during which a number of modifications to passenger areas were made, including revised luggage racks, space for a refreshment trolley and modifications to the toilets.

Traction power for the Gatwick Express trains was originally provided by standard Class 73/1 locomotives. At drawing board stage no technical alterations were planned for the locomotives, and it was envisaged that the Class 73s could be drawn from the general pool to cover the service; however, after only a short period this proved undesirable. The Class 73 was designed for use at one end (usually the Gatwick end) of each train; control at the opposite end was provided by a fleet of 10 GLV (Gatwick Luggage Vans), which were converted by BREL Eastleigh from redundant 2HAP MBSO vehicles. The 'new' GLV vehicles retained their traction equipment to supplement that of the Class 73 for traction, and also provided the auxiliary power supply to operate heat and light throughout the train. The rebuilding of the GLVs was a major undertaking, with the complete vehicle being gutted, new window and door positions cut, and the driving cab rebuilt, with a guard's (conductor's) office fitted at the inner end. Modifications also had to be made to the draw gear at the inner end, as a buck-eye coupling and side buffers were now required in place of the former centre buffer.

Although the Gatwick Express service was not operated under the InterCity flag until May 1985 all stock was finished in the then Executive, or Main Line colour scheme. To mark the launch of the Gatwick express service, locomotive No 73123 was also outshopped in the Executive colours and named *Gatwick Express*. The GE stock which was converted jointly by BREL Derby Litchurch Lane and Eastleigh was delivered to the SR from Autumn 1983, and commissioned at Strawberry Hill Depot before being transferred to the Gatwick Express depot at Stewarts Lane.

Below: During 'peak' periods and the summer months nine-vehicle sets were always used, thus giving accommodation for 41 first- and 336 standard-class passengers (originally, seating was provided for 386 standard customers). Being unusually 'led' in the up direction by the Electro-Diesel, the 09.20 Gatwick Airport-Victoria of 18 April 1985 clears Streatham North Junction with No 73138 at the helm. *Author*

Above: The 10 Gatwick Luggage Vans (GLVs) were rebuilt by BREL Eastleigh from redundant Class 414 (HAP) MBSO vehicles, very little of the original coaches remaining, except for the front end and underframe. GLV No 9106 rebuilt from HAP MBSO No 61299 (unit No 6101) leads the 14.05 Gatwick Airport-Victoria towards Clapham Junction on 14 May 1984 – the first day of public service. *Author*

Once sufficient stock was delivered a major driver and staff training programme commenced, and this was followed by numerous running-in turns, taking the Gatwick Express formations to a number of South Coast and South Western Division locations.

The big day for the new London-Gatwick service was 14 May 1984 when the 15 minute interval, 30-minute journey time Gatwick Express commenced operation. The 15-minute service originally operated between 05.30 and 22.30, while an hourly service worked during the night hours. Revisions due to changing traffic flows saw some amendments to the early morning and late evening service frequency. From service introduction trains were formed of a Class 73/1, two three-car and one two-car Class 488, plus a Class 489 GLV. The service got off to a very promising start, with encouraging loading figures. Regrettably after only a few weeks several serious locomotive fires befell the service, which culminated in the near-destruction of the SR flagship No 73142 *Broadlands* on 5 August 1984 at Battersea Park. This was by far the most serious incident and led to the 'blacking' of the service by train crews at Victoria Depot, until some sort of explanation could be found. The problem was traced to the locomotive's electrical system which, when encountering short gaps in the live rail at speed, had insufficient time to 'run-back' the power camshaft to a suitable start position, preventing the resurgence of power causing a large electric arc on the pick up shoes, which in turn could ignite dirt or grease on the underframe. While remedial action was being considered a revised Gatwick service operated, firstly utilising EMUs and later five-car Gatwick Express sets operated by two Class 73/1 locomotives in multiple under diesel power. This temporary operation continued for three weeks until fibreglass bogie guard 'arc shields' were fitted, and minor modifications made to locomotive control systems.

During the winter timetable, when airport passenger levels were at their lowest, the Gatwick Express service was modified, with five-car formations being the norm; however, over the Christmas period standard formations were used. By the spring of 1985 the SR announced that since the Gatwick Express service was launched a 32 per cent increase in line revenue had been recorded, with over 2.8 million people using the service during a 12-month period, this represented 40 per cent of the air travellers using Gatwick Airport.

By 1987 sufficient time had elapsed to calculate the lasting effect of the Gatwick Express service on the Class 73/1 fleet. Apart from increasing the annual mileage by 50 per cent, and a revision of the maintenance policy for the entire fleet, the locomotives had stood up well to the continued thrashing over the Victoria-Gatwick route.

In early 1988, following sectorisation, the decision was taken to identify 'dedicated' locomotives for the InterCity sponsored services. The best 12 locomotives were selected. Technically these were still Class 73/1s; however, from the summer of 1989 it was agreed, following the splitting up of the rail operations into accountable businesses, that the 12 locomotives would be reclassified as Class 73/2, and be fully maintained for 90mph operation and renumbered 73201-212. The remaining locomotives would only be maintained for 60mph running. The Class 73/2 fleet was eventually expanded by two; from April 1991 No 73135 was reclassified as a 73/2 and renumbered 73235, and No 73112 was modified to 73213 in July 1996. Originally No 73235 was drafted in to cover for No 73205, which was on long-term loan to European Passenger Services for traction current development work with former Class 33 No 33115, which was mounted on Eurostar-style bogies.

In 1992 it was decided that to retain vacuum brake exhausters and vacuum brake control equipment on the InterCity locomotives was an expensive luxury which could be dispensed with.

Above: On 5 August 1984, No 73142 was seriously damaged by fire at Battersea Park, while hauling a Gatwick Express service. The problem, which took several days to trace, was found to be a gap in the live rail only slightly longer than the locomotive; as the locomotive regained power from the gap, severe arcing occurred which started the fire. While the problem was being solved, pairs of Class 73/1s operating under diesel conditions were used to power five-car formations. Nos 73111/117 haul the 10.30 Victoria - Gatwick Airport past Coulsdon North on 7 August. *Author*

Since virtually no vacuum stock remained in traffic and the InterCity locomotives should not be required to haul freight trains, the vacuum brake systems were progressively isolated from mid-1992. The first locomotive to have the vacuum equipment removed was No 73212 following a classified overhaul at BRML Eastleigh in December 1993.

From October 1993, the InterCity Gatwick Express commenced operation as the first of the shadow franchise companies. This gave the business far more control of its operations and assets. In December 1993, the new Managing Director, Rob Mason, relaunched the service. The most striking change was new staff uniforms, and a slight re-livery of the stock and locomotives. On the locomotives the red/white waist height banding of the InterCity livery was replaced by a narrow burgundy band,

Below: During the period of livery transition, much discussion took place over what colours the locomotives should carry for the service. The Executive or InterCity colours were always firm favourite to match the stock. No 73123 nears Horley with the 14.30 from Victoria on 30 August 1984, with the target No 2 on the front. *Author*

while the 'Gatwick Express' legend replaced the InterCity markings on the locomotives' upper body panels. The coaches also lost their red/white side bands in favour of a burgundy band and the legend 'Gatwick Express'. The GLVs also carried the new Gatwick Express logo on the front end above the headcode panel. By early 1995, all Class 73/2s had been repainted into the latest Gatwick Express livery.

The privatisation of the Gatwick Express operation came in April 1996 when a 15-year franchise was awarded to the National Express Group. The length of the franchise permitted time to plan and develop the present and future service aimed at carrying 40 million customers annually by 2008.

One of the first major tasks was to plan for new rolling stock as the 1950s and 1960s technology could not be refurbished any further. It was therefore agreed to invite competitive tenders for a fleet of new multiple-unit trains. The winning design was a derivative of the Alstom 'Juniper' EMU classified 460. These elegant futuristic styled sets with very streamlined front ends and quality passenger accommodation included a dedicated luggage van at the London end of each formation. The sets were built at the Alstom factory at Washwood Heath, Birmingham, and delivered in 2000/01.

Huge problems with the introduction of the 'Juniper' stock ensured that the ED and mark 2 formations remained running well beyond the original date of replacement.

Between 2000-2004 the majority of Class 73/2s and Class 488 passenger sets were retired, leaving just a couple of sets to provide emergency cover until the summer of 2005 when on 28 July the final Class 73-powered train made a ceremonial journey over the Victoria-Gatwick route. However in true railway tradition this was not the real end and on several occasions the sole remaining GE Class 73 No 73202 made appearances on the line up until the end of the year.

The displaced stock and locomotives, by now owned by Porterbrook Leasing were returned after withdrawal to the lease owner. Most Class 73s have subsequently found further use, while the Class 488 and 489s have either been scrapped, entered departmental service, especially as test train 'make-up' vehicles or entered the world of preservation.

Below: The Class 73 retained by Gatwick Express following full introduction of Class 460s, No 73202 *Dave Berry*, was modified by Stewarts Lane to include a bodyside indicator light used to provide a visual indication of door release when attached to a Class 460 'Juniper' unit. No 73202 is seen in July 2005 at Gatwick Airport. *Author*

Right: In December 1993, following the formation of separately accountable train operating units within the main BR framework in readiness for privatisation, the Gatwick Express locomotives started to be repainted in the new business identity. This followed InterCity colours, but sported a new Gatwick Express logo on the body side in place of the InterCity legend and a burgundy band in place of the red. The first locomotive to sport the livery was No 73206 *Gatwick Express*, seen at Gatwick Airport on 15 December 1993. *Author*

Above: To mark the final demise of locomotive-hauled operation of the Gatwick Express service, National Express Group and local management agreed to a special event on 28 July 2005 when the 12.15 Victoria-Gatwick Airport and 13.00 return would be formed of the last two operational Class 73/2s, Nos 73202 and 73208 working 'top and tail' with a Class 488/489 formation. Led by No 73208, the last booked southbound ED-powered Gatwick Express passes Clapham Junction. Since the service began in May 1984 over 440,000 Class 73 powered Gatwick Express trains departed from London Victoria. *Brian Morrison*

The 'Big' Electro-Diesels Class 74

odernisation and electrification of the Waterloo-Bournemouth route west of Pirbright Junction during the mid-1960s led to the introduction of the 10 'Big EDs' or Class 74s. With electrification to Bournemouth and the introduction of quick-acceleration high-powered EMUs on most services between the two points, other core traffic, principally boat-train services to/from Southampton Docks, which also had to traverse non-electrified sections of line, would cause major pathing problems if lighter-powered diesel locomotives were used.

Southern Region operators and design engineers from the Brighton drawing office studied the problem for many months. The most desirable option would have been to use pairs of production Class 73/1s; this would have given 3,200hp under electric conditions, which was on-par with the REP EMUs used on the fast passenger services, while 1,200hp would have been available for diesel operation. This would have easily shifted passenger train loads of between 10-13 vehicles over non-electrified dock lines. However, commitments for the 'JB' or Class

73/1s could not release 20 machines for this work.

At around the same time, a downturn in electric locomotive requirements on the Southern's Eastern Division of the Kent Coast electrified network led to several of the 1950s Doncaster-built E5000 locomotives (Class 71) becoming spare. The South Western section engineers immediately saw potential in obtaining these and delved into various possibilities of reuse as an electric or dual-power locomotive were studied. Eventually, in collaboration with English Electric and the BR Workshops Division a package was put together to rebuild a batch of 10 Class 71s into 'big' electro-diesels, classified 74.

Rebuilding the locomotives for dual-power operation was a major undertaking which was contracted to Crewe Locomotive Works. The locomotives were completely gutted down to their main component parts with the sides and cab sections removed from the original underframe, which was extensively rebuilt. In reality the depth of rebuilding was more-time consuming and costly than building new locomotives.

Below: Totally stripped down to a bare frame and side members, the body shell from former straight electric E5015 is seen inside the fabrication shop at BR Crewe Works in July 1966. The level of work undertaken on these body shells in conversion to electro-diesels was probably more expensive than ordering brand new locomotives. When this view was taken the new skeleton side frame was installed together with the mid-body-length air louvres. When returned to traffic No E5015 became the first of the Class 74 fleet, No E6101. *Author's Collection*

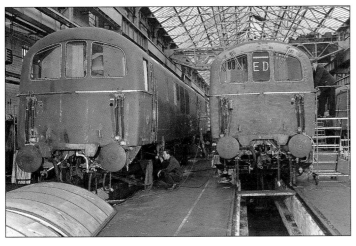

Above: Once the frame had been upgraded and the new bodysides and cabs had been fitted in the fabrication area, the Class 74 rebuild work was transferred to the main erecting shop, where around eight locomotives were under rebuild at the same time. In this view Nos E6104 and E6106 take shape. No E6104 in the background already has its cab handrails fitted, while No E6106 is little more than a shell. *Author's Collection*

Left: In an advanced state near completion, Nos E6102 and E6103 stand side by side in the main erecting shop. No E6102 on the right was awaiting space in the test house and then the paint shop before final inspection and delivery to the Southern. *Author's Collection*

Below: In immaculate ex-paint shop condition, No E6105, rebuilt from No E5019, poses in the works yard at Crewe Works for official pictures on 9 February 1968. It is interesting to record the length of time some of these locomotives were under conversion, with works records showing that this one took 14 months to rebuild, test and paint. Note the overhead warning signs are fitted to the handrails rather than the body. *Author's Collection*

To provide smooth operation in their days as electric locomotives the Class 71s or 'HAs' incorporated a flywheel and booster set, enabling a constant supply of power to the traction motors when running over small gaps in the live rail. For their 'new' role this was deemed unnecessary, but the booster set was retained and formed an integral unit with the traction motor blowers. Auxiliary power for the new fleet came from a Paxman 'Ventura' 6YJXL engine, set to delivery 650hp. This was a fast running power unit of a type already in use on BR in the Class 14 0-6-0 diesel-hydraulic fleet. In being a fast-running engine, the generator could be small and light, a very important aspect of the design when limited space was available.

The total redesign of the locomotives to operate from both electric and diesel power sources caused a significant weight increase over the original design; for this reason, a dismantle of the body structure was needed, as the side sections had to be strengthened to become load bearing, this was achieved by

Above: One of the regular working for the Class 74s following delivery right through until withdrawal in 1977 was on the then nightly Newspaper trains from Waterloo to Bournemouth and Poole. In the days when the daily news media was printed in London and transported to the regions three nightly paper trains departed from Waterloo. On 17 October 1974, No 74009 awaits the signal to depart with the 02.15 to Bournemouth. To speed delivery in the west newspapers would be sorted *en route* and bundled for shop delivery. *Brian Morrison*

inserting a warren girder framework. It was also easier to amend the body design and incorporate new window and louvre positions with the structures off the frame.

Internal design of the new locomotives consisted of a full-width driving cab at both ends; the driving seat was in the standard left position with a fold-down assistant's seat on the right. Behind the cab was a full-width walkway with doors on both sides. From the walkway was a door providing access into the equipment and engine room. The equipment area housed a cooler group, control equipment, booster unit and the engine/generator group. It was basically one large compartment providing all-round access to the engine generator and booster.

In many ways the '74s' were a futuristic design, with a special place in rail traction history. English Electric, the main sub-contractor for this build, decided to install a 'closed loop' electrical control system; this allowed the driver to select any desired value of acceleration current which was maintained automatically up to

the limit of the locomotive's performance. There were major advantages using this method of control over the more usual resistance type, and experience showed a major increase in tractive effort in any given rail condition. The 'closed loop' system also assisted in tractive effort control when operating under diesel conditions. At the time of construction the electronics and solid-state control equipment was used for the first time and was the most advanced on any locomotive in the UK, and in many ways served as a prototype for subsequent designs.

Conversion of the 10 worst-condition Class 71s was a protracted affair at Crewe, with the first locomotive of the fleet delivered to Stewarts Lane in November 1967 after 13 months under conversion. The final locomotive of the build, No E6110, was not delivered until June 1968. On the Southern Region, as the '74s' were to be deployed on the Waterloo-Bournemouth route their home shed was Eastleigh, although most commissioning and some maintenance was carried out at Stewarts Lane.

Above: Apart from powering boat trains between Waterloo and Southampton/Bournemouth and overnight Newspaper trains, the Class 74s could be found powering all kinds of secondary duties. Here on 17 June 1972 No E6106 storms past Surbiton hauling a 4TC unit from Bournemouth to Chart Leacon. The '74' powered the set as far as Stewarts Lane, as drivers on the South Eastern section were not trained on Class 74 operation. *Author*

Below: Viewed from the British Telecom building adjacent to the tight curve at Vauxhall, No 74007 traverses the 'down Windsor' line with the 09.57 Waterloo to Clapham Junction empty stock move on 18 September 1974. The stock on this train had arrived in the capital with the first 'up' service from Yeovil Junction. *John Scrace*

The number range allocated to the conversions was E6101-E6110 and while classified 74 under the BR numeric system, on the Southern Region the locomotives were more usually known as HBs. From new the entire fleet was painted in standard BR corporate rail blue, offset by black underframes and full yellow warning ends - a livery which remained until the fleet was withdrawn.

Unlike the 'small EDs' or Class 73s, the driving cab layout of the '74s' was not favoured by many staff. It was distinctly 1950s and remained virtually unchanged from its days as an all electric machine. Power under both main (electric) and auxiliary (diesel) conditions was controlled by one handle on the driver's right side, which moved from an off position at approximately the 11 o'clock mark, to full power at the seven o'clock position. On the driver's left side were two brake controllers, one a straight air valve for the locomotive's independent brake, and the other a proportional valve controlling either air or vacuum train brakes with proportional application on the locomotive. All air, traction and speed displays were desk-mounted with switching located below the two-character route indicator.

On the driver's assistant side a secondary power controller (not physically linked to the main controller) was provided, as were train and locomotive brake valves, a DSD hold-over button and limited auxiliary controls. The presence of the duplicate controls - requested on the original build - greatly assisted in shunting duties and were especially useful when working through Southampton Docks where often parked motor vehicles were left very close to the rail lines and the driver having the ability to work from both sides of the cab saved several accidents.

During the rebuild work, the original front layout was largely retained; however, buck-eye couplings and Pullman rubbing plates were fitted together with rotating Oleo retractable buffers. Body-mounted waist-height air pipes and multiple control jumpers were also added, enabling full multiple operation with Class 33/1, 73 and 1951, 1957, 1963 and 1966 classic EMUs.

The rebuilding work also extended to the bogies, where major changes were made to the secondary springing. In addition retractable third-rail pick-up shoes were added, these being air lowered and spring raised.

When operating under electric conditions there was little to surpass the performance of a Class 74, with 2,552hp under control

of the 'closed loop' system. On diesel power the Paxman 'Ventura' of 650hp output was more than adequate to lift passenger trains through Southampton Docks or indeed on the main line if the power supply was interrupted. One of the biggest problems with the fleet was getting the diesel and booster set to run, with both English Electric and SR electrical engineers spending hundreds of hours trying to sort out problems with the solid state control equipment. The engine was started in the conventional way, which also operated the air compressor to build up main reservoir air pressure; when sufficient was available, a trip switch closed, allowing the booster to run at high speed and together with the engine provided a traction output. This arrangement also needed an almost full header tank of coolant water which was also controlled by solid state electronics and was a constant problem.

The author has strong memories of working on this fleet of locomotives and spending lengthy periods standing in the engine room either with a bucket of water trying to top up the header tank via a hand pump, or generally coaxing the engine/booster set to life.

Another problem from which the fleet suffered was 'bounce'. This was principally generated by the uneven weight distribution. When 'bounce' started, it was difficult to stop and on more than one occasion a driver has had to stop his train to stop the rocking. Normally the 'bounce' was induced by poor track conditions.

When introduced the principal deployment of the fleet was on Waterloo Southampton/Bournemouth passenger, mail, van and empty stock duties, working daily into Southampton Docks and often using their auxiliary power for shunting. On their intended duties performance was excellent, consistently working 400+ ton trains in excess of 90mph, as well as plodding 'off the juice' into Southampton East or West Docks right up to the side of ocean liners.

When the Southampton Docks passenger traffic decreased the fleet were deployed on some freight duties, one turn often worked was the nightly Southampton-South Lambeth vacuum fitted freight. This train, usually loaded between 800-1,000 tons, departed from Southampton at 04.03 travelling via Basingstoke, Woking, Staines and Clapham Junction, arriving at South Lambeth soon after 06.00. This duty taxed the class to their limits with often the Paxman engine being hardly able to shift the load out of the docks on arduous rail conditions.

Left: As the years progressed it was quite surprising how many freight duties crept into the duties of the Class 74s; even more so given the limited number of drivers trained on the fleet's operation, principally top link men at Waterloo, Woking, Basingstoke, Eastleigh and Bournemouth. On 14 May 1971 No E6106 is seen near Winchester powering a Bevois Park (Southampton) to Halling cement train. The Class 74 was rostered to power this service as far as South Lambeth, from where a South Eastern section Class 33 would be provided to continue the journey. *Author*

Right: One of the most unusual and taxing duties given to the Class 74s was on coal traffic between Wimbledon and Acton Yard, where the 600hp Paxman diesel had to provide all the power to lift a train of up to 700 tonnes over the West London line through Brompton, Kensington Olympia and North Pole Junction. On 14 August 1973 No E6107 powers the 14.20 Acton-Wimbledon past West Brompton. This train would recess at Wimbledon West before continuing to Tolworth and Chessington at 03.55 and 05.55 the following day. Note the brake tender coupled behind the locomotive. *John Scrace*

During the 1970s, with more spare locomotives available, the class became regular motive power for the Chessington/Tolworth-Acton coal trains. These were routed via Wimbledon, Streatham and Clapham Junction, having to use the diesel output all the way from Clapham to Acton via Kensington Olympia and the now closed connection with the GW main line at North Pole Junction. The gradients of this route, compounded by shunting requests at Acton, often took its toll on the class, with failures occurring almost weekly. If problems occurred while at Acton, the Western Region authorities would have the locomotive, complete with Southern Region crew hauled to Old Oak Common; here the Old Oak train crew supervisor would stand guard over the Southern men ensuring they didn't run away, as nobody on the then Western Region could either drive or had any knowledge of the fleet.

With the general decline in traffic, compounded by their unreliability, the Southern M&EE decided to phase the locomotives out of service in 1976. By early that year it was agreed that no further heavy general overhauls would be undertaken and that locomotives long out of traffic with serious faults and damage would not be repaired. This mainly affected No 74006, which had lain at Eastleigh Works since mid-1975 with fire damage received at Battledown flyover, west of Basingstoke, while heading a boat train to London.

The run-down of the class was assisted by the ever-reducing locomotive requirement on the Southern and the redeployment of other assets, namely the Class 73s. The final few Class 74s were taken out of service at Christmas 1977.

One locomotive worthy of special note was No E6104; this was fitted with a prototype Southern Region Automatic Warning System, which for the first time brought actual signal aspects into the driving cab. The signal approaching was displayed on a panel on the left side, while the signal aspect previously past was displayed on the right side. This equipment was operated by track inductive loops which were installed in the New Forest and between Esher and New Malden. The system served as a major development tool for future AWS and cab warning systems.

Sadly, although a number of locomotives were in quite good condition and left stored at Eastleigh for a considerable time, none were preserved, a major loss to the overall preservation of modern traction.

Class 74 Technical Data

Class:	74	Coupling restriction:	Blue Star (Note: 1)
Number range:	74001-74010	Brake force:	41 tonnes
Original number range:	E6101-E6110, rebuilt from Class 71	Nominal power supply:	600-750V dc
Rebuilt by:	BR Workshops Crewe	Engine type:	Paxman 6YJXL
Introduced:	1966-68	Horsepower (Electric):	2,552hp
Wheel arrangement:	Bo-Bo	(Diesel):	650hp
Weight (operational):	86 tonnes	Rail horsepower (Electric):	2,020hp
Height:	12ft 9 ⁵/₈in	(Diesel):	315hp
Width:	9ft 0in	Tractive effort (Electric):	47,500lb
Length (Buffers extended):	50ft 5 ³/₄in	(Diesel):	40,000lb
(Buffers retracted):	49ft 3 ³/₄in	Cylinder bore:	7in
Min curve negotiable:	4 chains	Cylinder stroke:	7 ³/₄in
Maximum speed:	90mph	Main generator type:	EE843
Wheel base:	37ft 6in	Traction motors:	4 x EE532A
Bogie wheel base:	10ft 6in	Gear ratio:	76:22
Bogie pivot centres:	27ft 0in	Fuel tank capacity:	310gals
Wheel diameter:	4ft 0in		
Brake type:	Dual		
Sanding equipment:	Pneumatic		
Heating type:	Electric - Index 66		
Route availability:	7		

Height: 12ft 9 5/8in
Length (Buffers extended): 50ft 5 3/4in
(Buffers retracted): 49ft 3 3/4in
Cylinder stroke: 7 3/4in

Note 1:
Blue Star multiple unit equipment was fitted for diesel operation. Locomotives were also able to operate in multiple under electric conditions with Class 73s and post-1951 EMUs up to and including 1966 stock.

Left: Most days between 1968 and 1976 a Class 74 could be found stabled at Waterloo during the day, either parked up in the North Sidings or the 'docks' between platforms 11 and 12. Adjacent to these dock roads was where the Waterloo shunting staff had their accommodation and where watering facilities existed for locomotives fitted with steam heating boilers. On 14 June 1974 No 74003 stands in No 2 dock, waiting for the ground signal to clear to make attachment to the 09.55 boat train to Weymouth. The Class 74 would work this service to Bournemouth, where it would be replaced by a Class 33/1. *Author*

Left: Class 74 driver's cab position. The cabs could be best described as spartan, with only a fold-down seat for the driver's assistant. The driver's desk housed the straight air brake and train brake valves on the left side, with the power controller on the right. The two press buttons in front of the brake controllers operated a high-speed vacuum-release feature and an anti-slip brake. The inclined display desk housed the usual instruments, while the metal handle at the far end behind the brake operated the sanding equipment. The cab from No 74003 is shown. *Author*

Class 74 Fleet List

BR 1957 No.	TOPS No.	Date re No.	Original Class 71 No.	Rebuilt by	Date Introduced	Depot of first allocation	Date withdrawn	Depot of final allocation	Disposal	Disposal detail	Date cut up
E6101	74001	12/73	E5015	BR Crewe	03/68	73A	12/77	EH	Cut up	Birds, Long Marston	08/78
E6102	74002	02/74	E5016	BR Crewe	11/67	73A	06/77	EH	Cut up	J Cashmore, Newport	12/77
E6103	74003	02/74	E5006	BR Crewe	01/68	73A	12/77	EH	Cut up	J Cashmore, Newport	12/80
E6104	74004	12/73	E5024	BR Crewe	03/68	73A	12/77	EH	Cut up	Birds, Long Marston	08/78
E6105	74005	12/73	E5019	BR Crewe	03/68	73A	12/77	EH	Cut up	BR Fratton, by Pounds	01/81
E6106	74006	02/74	E5023	BR Crewe	04/68	73A	06/76	EH	Cut up	G Cohen, Kettering	06/77
E6107	74007	02/74	E5003	BR Crewe	04/68	73A	12/77	EH	Cut up	Birds, Long Marston	08/78
E6108	74008	02/74	E5005	BR Crewe	05/68	73A	12/77	EH	Cut up	Birds, Long Marston	08/78
E6109	74009	01/74	E5017	BR Crewe	05/68	73A	12/77	EH	Cut up	Birds, Long Marston	08/78
E6110	74010	02/74	E5021	BR Crewe	06/68	73A	12/77	EH	Cut up	BREL Doncaster	10/79

Right: The main depot for the Class 74s was Eastleigh, where depot space was shared with Classes 03, 07, 08, 09 and 33, together with a sizeable variety of visiting motive power of virtually any class. With a lack of booked turns, compounded by frequent failures, the depot was usually host to at least three Class 74s at most times.
On 10 October 1976 No 74001 stands in Eastleigh Airport Sidings with Class 08s Nos 08845/854, Class 07s Nos 07009/013 and 4TC No 434.
Brian Morrison

Below: Displaying the headcode '1E', Class 74 No 74010 heads through Eastleigh station on the 'down' main line on 3 May 1976, with a short fitted freight for Southampton Eastern Docks.
Brian Morrison

Electro-Diesel Maintenance

Above: No 73105 painted in 'more yellow' livery stands outside the electric shed at Stewarts Lane Depot, the home for the 73s. The two right-hand lines are full length, while that on the left, obscured by the locomotive, is a short line, able to accommodate just one locomotive. *Author*

Following assembly of the six prototype locomotives at Eastleigh Carriage Works, tests and commissioning were conducted at Eastleigh Depot. After authorisation was given the fleet took up allocation at Stewarts Lane Depot in South London, a site easily accessible from all three divisions of the Southern Region. The Stewarts Lane facility consisted of a three-track electric shed, which was already home to the Class 71s.

The three-road electric shed had two full-length (five-locomotive) and one short (single-locomotive) length tracks, and was responsible for all exams. Lifting facilities and pits were also provided and from the late 1970s a wheel lathe was installed. Stewarts Lane depot also had a two-track diesel shed where the EDs of both classes received service exams and fuel. The centre of the Stewarts Lane complex consisted of a carriage depot principally designed for EMUs but in later years, following closure of the EWS facility, became the home for the Gatwick Express operation.

When delivered the Class 74s were allocated to Eastleigh Depot, thus being close to the Bournemouth-Waterloo line on which they worked. Both Stewarts Lane and Eastleigh shared responsibilities for both classes of electro-diesel with Class 74s frequently found at Stewarts Lane and '73's at Eastleigh. In latter years some Class 73s were allocated for a short period to Eastleigh and following the

demise of Stewarts Lane the EWS allocation was transferred to Hither Green.

Other depots which frequently dealt with Class 73s included Ashford and Hither Green on the Eastern Section, Selhurst, Norwood, and Brighton on the Central Division and Bournemouth on the Western side.

Main works overhauls until the 1970s were undertaken by Crewe, this being transferred later to Eastleigh. In later years classified attention was carried out at Selhurst Level 5 Depot. For many years from the late 1960s until the late 1980s Slade Green was the principal accident repair facility on the Southern Region.

Under privatisation the Class 73s, being a rather unusual breed, remained principally south of the Thames; however, Toton Depot did review a pair in the early EWS years and likewise Brush Traction, Loughborough were invited to inspect a pair of locomotives in the view of a refurbishment scheme.

The four Class 73/0s transferred to Merseyrail were allocated to Birkenhead North but also received attention at Hall Road.

Today FM Rail is the principal maintainer of the remaining operational Class 73s for GBRf, Network Rail and European passenger services. The SWT-allocated locomotives receive attention at East Wimbledon Depot and are fuelled at Salisbury.

Above: During the 1970s and 1980s, around five members of the Class 73 fleet at one time could be found receiving programmed maintenance at Stewarts Lane. However, the position largely changed in the depot's closing years, with many diesel classes receiving attention in the one-time home of the EDs. In this view, the line-up, from nearest the camera consists of Nos 73119, 73005, 73102, 73123, and No 73118 on the left. *Author*

Right middle: Adjacent to Stewarts Lane Electric Depot was the carriage and wagon shop, where a number of traffic and departmental wagons and coaches were repaired. In later years the three-road building was used for specialist repair, rebuilding, and painting work for BR and Mainline Freight. On several occasions the building acted as a paint shop to prepare Class 73s prior to naming, or powering special services. In this view on 3 June 1985, the flagship of the fleet No 73142 *Broadlands* receives its New InterCity colours prior to operating a Royal train. *Author*

Right: Although officially allocated to Eastleigh, the Class 74s received daily service checks at Stewarts Lane and Bournemouth Depots. Here No 74010 stands inside the two-track diesel servicing depot at Stewarts on 17 June 1977 after arriving in the capital at the head of the Weymouth-Waterloo Channel Island boat train. After working empty stock to Clapham Junction yard the '74' visited Stewarts Lane for fuel and water, prior to returning to Waterloo in preparation for working the down evening Channel Island express boat train. *Author*

Above: Since their introduction in the 1960s, classified overhauls have only been carried out at two BREL establishments, Eastleigh and Crewe; the latter only for a short period in the late 1960s when reorganisation was being carried out at Eastleigh, as well as Selhurst Level 5 Depot in the late-1980s. Class 73/0 No 73005 is seen perched on accommodation stands at BREL Eastleigh on 25 April 1984. When this locomotive emerged it was repainted in the 'more yellow' scheme. *Author*

Left: During the course of their lives very few collisions occurred to the Class 73s. One that did require major surgery was No 73132, which collided with a Motorail vehicle at Eastleigh in February 1980. The front end was badly pushed in, necessitating new front panelling. Repairs were carried out at the then SR's collision repair depot at Slade Green, and by the end of the year the locomotive was back in service. *Author*

Below: In 1996, Class 73/1 No 73111 was withdrawn from service and stripped of all re-usable components at Stewarts Lane, thus providing a spare pair of bogies and other equipment for the then current refurbishment programme. A shortage of spare parts had been a long-time problem with heavy maintenance of the class. The locomotive is seen awaiting its final fate on 28 August 1996. *Author*

Right: Soon after English Welsh & Scottish (EWS) purchased the three UK freight operators under the privatisation of the UK railway, a refurbishment plan was drawn up for a handful of Class 73s, with the work scheduled to be undertaken at Stewarts Lane. As time came to prove only two locomotives were completed before the decision to phase the class out emerged under an EWS traction-rationalisation plan. The second of the refurbished locomotives, No 73131, is seen with its body prepared for repainting at Stewarts Lane on 20 August 1996, while behind is 'Pullman' No 73101, which at the time was planned to be the third locomotive of the refurbishment project. On the right in the distance is No 73126. *Author*

Middle: National Express Group and Porterbrook Leasing contracted Wessex Traincare at Eastleigh to carry-out classified attention to the Class 73/2 fleet, following the demise of the Level 5 facility at Selhurst. On 23 December 1996 No 73235 is seen inside the main erecting shop at Eastleigh receiving a general overhaul. *Author*

Below: Until the introduction of component exchange maintenance the Class 73s visited main works every four or five years for classified attention; however, if major problems befell a member within this time, it would receive casual attention. Over the years, with the SR operating heavy repair workshops at Selhurst and Slade Green, these have tended to cater for the un-programmed repairs. Receiving an Intermediate overhaul at Selhurst Level 5 Depot, Class 73/1 No 73119 is seen on depot supports, while another of the class is on the left. No 73119 was released from this overhaul painted in 'Dutch' livery. *Author*

Above: Empty Coaching Stock duties between Waterloo and Clapham Yard featured largely in the Class 73 diagrams until these were dispensed with in the late 1980s. With its third-rail collector shoes in the raised position, No 73119 stands in Platform 11 at Waterloo on 18 January 1983, forming the 10.14 empties to Clapham Yard. The stock had arrived in the capital with a service from Yeovil Junction. *Author*

Below: By the early 1990s van trains were a thing of the past at Waterloo, with newspaper, mail and parcels traffic transferred to road haulage. During the mid-1980s a Sunday afternoon parcels train operated, departing Waterloo at 16.55 for Bournemouth. It is seen in the old platform 15 at Waterloo on 19 April 1985, powered by 'more yellow'-liveried No 73140, formed of just two GUV vehicles. *Author*

Above: With a fairly small fleet of less than 50 locomotives, having two Class 73-hauled trains in one picture is quite unusual, and for them both to have such short trains was even more of an advantage to the photographer. In this view at Clapham Junction, taken on 13 August 1981, No 73124 on the left hauls the SR route training saloon No ADM395280, while approaching the station on the down main line, No 73111 heads two coaches bound for BREL Eastleigh Works for classified attention. *Author*

Below: Parked in the old platform 15 at Waterloo station, long before the mid-station office block was removed and the International Station built, Class 74 No 74003 awaits departure time with the 21.36 Waterloo-Eastleigh van train, carrying Royal Mail and parcels traffic on 20 October 1977, just two months before the remaining operational class members were withdrawn. *Author*

Above: Whenever the 1940-built Waterloo & City line stock was required to visit a main line depot, complicated transfer arrangements had to be made, as the W&C cars needed to be marshalled between special 'Ward' coupling-fitted match wagons, and locomotive-hauled. On 22 September 1983, W&C trailer No S78 was moved from Waterloo to Selhurst. Motive power was provided by Class 73 No 73135 and the train is seen at Wimbledon South sidings, awaiting a crew change. *Author*

Left upper: During the introduction of the Class 455s in the early 1980s uncommissioned sets were not permitted to operate under their own power, therefore all pre-commissioning moves had to be locomotive-operated. The position was further complicated as the sets were not compatible with locomotive couplings, necessitating the provision of match wagons. No 73112 hauls Class 455/7 No 5705 through Clapham Cutting on 18 July 1984 with a transfer move between East Wimbledon Depot and Clapham Yard. *Author*

Right middle: With Wimbledon Park EMU depot on the right, housing an all-blue-liveried 4VEP and a 1957-design 4EPB. Class 74 No E6110 passes by on the up fast line on 26 June 1970 powering a daytime Southampton Western Docks-Waterloo parcels train formed of a mix of ex Southern, LMS and BR van types. *Author*

Left below: Even after the full fleet of 'Wessex' Class 442 units were available, some of the Waterloo-Bournemouth duties were operated for a short period by either single or pairs of Class 73s with TC stock. On 6 March 1989 the 06.55 Poole-Waterloo passes Wimbledon, powered by Nos 73112 and 73130. *Author*

Right: Class 73s were regularly deployed on weekend engineering duties, where their dual power was useful, being able to operate trains between yards and work sites under electric power, and then carry-out 'on site' duties using their diesel traction. Two locomotives, Nos 73108 and 73104, are seen at Wimbledon West on 24 October 1982 during track relaying work. *Author*

Above: The use of double-headed EDs in the BR operating days was never common, but after privatisation this became a more common sight. On 24 April 1984, to balance overnight diagrams, the 08.45 Eastleigh down carriage siding to Clapham Yard empty van service was double-headed by Nos 73102 and 73125, and is captured between New Malden and Raynes Park. *Author*

Left middle: Taken on 16 December 1977, only days before withdrawal, Class 74 No 74005 and a 4TC unit were used on a most unusual service, forming the shuttle connection between Weybridge and Staines via Chertsey. The deployment of the locomotive with its 600hp diesel was required due to a major power failure which took several hours to rectify. The train is seen in the bay platform at Weybridge. The locomotive for this train was provided from Waterloo and the TC 'pinched' from an off-peak Waterloo-Bournemouth service. *Ray Ruffell*

Left below: After heavy overnight snow in the South of England, and a major permanent way operation near Surbiton, services on the Waterloo main line were seriously disrupted on Sunday 6 January 1985. Class 73 No 73132, with a long departmental-engineers' train, awaits the signal between Berrylands and Surbiton, while 4TC No 404 leads a Waterloo-Bournemouth service travelling 'down' the 'up' fast line. *Author*

Above: The SR 1930s-built Surbiton station is the setting for the 07.30 Weymouth Quay-Waterloo boat train headed by No 73102 on 21 June 1984. Surbiton Station became one of the few 'modern' pieces of railway architecture to be 'listed' with effect from the end of 1985. *Brian Morrison*

Right: For a short period in the summer of 1980 the 17.34 Waterloo-Basingstoke service was formed of locomotive-hauled stock and diagrammed for a Class 73. This was due to an acute shortage of suitable EMUs. On 9 May 1980, to balance locomotive diagrams, the train was double-headed by Class 73 Nos 73111 and 73141, and is seen approaching Surbiton. *Author*

Left: One of the main South West Division's permanent-way engineers' yards in BR days, and indeed today under the privatised railway, is located at Woking, 25 miles from the capital. A large number of departmental trains are often found in this area, particularly at weekends. On 8 June 1984 'more yellow' No 73138 pulls into Woking station with a rake of empty 'Turbot' wagons from Farnham ballast tip. *Author*

Right: One of the most popular duties performed by the Class 74s for many years was the Waterloo-Bournemouth leg of the twice daily Waterloo-Weymouth Quay Channel Island boat trains. These services, formed of up to 10 Mk1 and Mk2 coaches complete with a buffet car, ran fast from Weymouth Quay to Bournemouth and then fast to Waterloo. On 3 June 1977 No 74005 approaches Woking with the 16.00 Weymouth Quay-Waterloo. *Author*

Below: With Woking station complex in the background, and the 'up' yard on the left, No 73139 hauls two coaches past Woking Junction on 9 April 1981, forming the Thursdays only 11.10 Clapham Yard to BREL Eastleigh Works stock transfer train. On the 'up' main line a 4REP/4TC/4TC set forms a Bournemouth-Waterloo fast service. *Author*

The *Electro-Diesels*

Above: The South West section's spoil tip was for many years located at Farnham on the Alton branch, and generated a small amount of ED traffic. No 73102 trundles a mix of 'Turbot', 'Tunney', and 'Plaice' wagons through St Johns cutting, west of Woking on 19 April 1984, bound for Farnham. *Author*

Below: Still sporting its 'as built' blue livery, with small yellow warning panel and grey roof, No E6029, which later became No 73122 and eventually No 73207, awaits the signal from Basingstoke on 22 February 1987, with a short un-fitted freight bound for Feltham Yard. *David Canning*

Above: Following classified overhaul at BREL Eastleigh Works, an active trial run was always operated before a locomotive was returned to revenue-earning traffic. This usually called for double-heading a service locomotive from Eastleigh as far as Clapham Junction. On 7 July 1981 ex-shops No 73107 piloted Class 33 No 33010 and is seen near Winchester Junction. *Author*

Left middle: Until the mid-1980s the recording of air-conditioned stock on the Southern Region was very rare, and this view of No 73139 approaching Eastleigh on 11 April 1985 with a full Eastern Region rake even made the railway press because of its rarity. The train was operated from Norwich Crown Point Depot to BREL Eastleigh for repainting into InterCity colours, prior to the new electrically-hauled services being introduced on the Liverpool Street-Norwich route the following month. *Author*

Left: The principal duties for which the Class 74s were converted, that of powering boat trains to and from Southampton Docks, were performed right up to the fleet's withdrawal in December 1977. Services linking London Waterloo with Southampton East and West Docks were much reduced in the 1970s with a considerably reduced number of ocean liners using the port, reflecting the increase in air travel. No 74010 prepares to run around its Mk1 rake of stock at Southampton Eastern Dock on 16 November 1977. *Author*

Above: No 73137 crosses from the 'down' main line via the 'up' main, and 'up' local line into Bevois Park Yard between St Denys and Southampton on 26 April 1985, hauling empty Motorail flats destined for Ford Transit traffic. *Author*

Right: Carrying the headcode '02' indicating that the train was bound for Clapham Junction yard, Class 74 No 75005 restarts an empty van train from the up platform at Eastleigh on 8 January 1976. In the down platform 4REP No 3014, one of 15 3,300hp tractor units used exclusively on the Waterloo-Bournemouth route is seen forming the power for the 12.46 Waterloo-Bournemouth service. *Philip D. Hawkins*

Above: It always caused a commotion when an ocean liner boat train traversed the railway system within Southampton Docks. Dock and railway staff, together with the police, were always on hand to assist in making sure the train had priority through the dual road / rail sections. On 12 August 1968, No E6009 pulls towards Canute Road on its way out of Southampton Eastern Docks with a boat express to Waterloo. *Alastair McIntyre*

Left: Another view of the same locomotive but this time on 1 May 1969. No E6009 was by now repainted with silver buffers and is seen on the rear of a 4TC returning empty from Southampton Eastern Docks to Eastleigh after forming a Royal Train from Waterloo. The train is seen at Canute Crossing, which signal box is on the left. *John H. Bird*

Above: The pairing of Class 73s and Class 33s was never common. However, on 10 August 1968, ED No E6020 pilots Class 33 No D6527 past Millbrook with a Waterloo-Bournemouth vans train.
Alastair McIntyre

Right: In preparation for the electrification of the Pirbright Junction-Bournemouth line a number of live rail clearance tests were carried out. Some used this unusual combination formed of an ex-SR design PUL driving car from set No 3031, a goods brake van and ED No E6043 operating on diesel power. This fascinating train is seen near Millbrook on 5 January 1967.
John H. Bird

Above: For much of the 1970s and 1980s, the SR and later Network SouthEast operated two staff route-training saloons that could be either hauled or propelled. Usually saloon No ADM395280 worked on the South Western section, while No ADS70155 operated on the Central and Eastern routes. No 73121 is seen in No 2 platform at Alton station on 20 July 1983 with saloon No ADM395280 *en route* to Clapham Junction. On the right Class 423 (4VEP) No 7720 awaits departure with the 12.50 to Waterloo. *Author*

Left: With a little thought a slightly different perspective from the standard front three-quarter view can be obtained at some locations. This picture was taken at Woking Junction on 9 April 1981 and came into the photographer's viewfinder totally by chance; as the rear of the shunt movement came into camera, No 73128 was approaching with a freight from Aldershot and Guildford bound for Woking. *Author*

Above: When the Southern Railway branch to Chessington was built in the mid-1930s, it was planned to continue the route onto Leatherhead via Malden Rushett. However, for many reasons, not least the outbreak of World War II, the line terminated at Chessington South. The tracks, however, continued past Chessington South station and served a local coal depot until the traffic was lost to road haulage in the late 1980s. No 73114 slowly departs from the coal yard bound for Wimbledon West Yard on 27 May 1981, during heavy rain, with empty 'housecoal' hoppers bound for South Wales via Acton. *Author*

Below: For many years the Southern Region testing section used the Farnham-Alton line for trials of new equipment. When the '74s' were delivered No E6102 was the subject of brake tests. Coupled with spare TC DTS No 76331 to carry instrumentation, the ED plied between Farnham and Alton at high speed to gauge the brake efficiency. The train is seen at Farnham carrying an appropriate 'HB' headcode. *Ray Ruffell*

Above: Perhaps a rather mundane duty for Main Line-liveried No 73103 was the Chipmans weed-control train, photographed at Thames Ditton on 17 May 1985 heading for Hampton Court. *Author*

Below: A freight diagram on the South Western section that was Class 73-operated for many years was the daily Bevois Park (Southampton)-Halling powder cement service, routed via the SWD main line, Chertsey, Staines, Richmond, Clapham Junction, and Factory Junction to gain the Eastern section lines. No 73107 passes Staines on 28 April 1984, with a rake of STS-owned PCA cement wagons. *Author*

Above: Not exactly what one would expect to find at Waterloo Station, a Class 74 and a six-wheel milk wagon! For many years the daily St Erth, Cornwall to Morden milk train conveyed one or two six-wheel wagons of milk for a processing plant at Vauxhall, London. This was 'tripped' from Clapham to the up Windsor loop line at Vauxhall for off-loading and then taken on to Waterloo to run around and return to Clapham for attachment to the overnight return empty milk train to St Erth. Class 74 No 74001 stands in Waterloo North Sidings on 13 March 1976 after arriving from Vauxhall. *Ray Ruffell*

Below: A rare meeting of two NSE-liveried Class 73s occurred at Ascot on 21 June 2001, when No 73129 on the right arrived on the tail of the 'Queen of Scots' Pullman train from Victoria conveying guests for the Royal Ascot race meeting. On the left, SWT 'Thunderbird' No 73109 arrives with 4VEP No 3405 as the 10.24 Aldershot-Ascot service, which was locomotive-hauled due to an AWS defect in the cab of the VEP unit. *Darren Ford*

Above & Below: From the spring of 1980 the Class 73 fleet became more intensely diagrammed than at any period since introduction, with the Gatwick Express passenger service and 'REP' fill-in duties while traction equipment was recovered from the REP stock for re-use on Class 442s. This required over 50 per cent of the fleet deployed on passenger services each weekday. The view above shows No 73129 hauling TCB No 2803 and TC No 8010 past St Johns, Woking with the 09.00 Bournemouth-Waterloo on 10 April 1987. The illustration below is of No 73106 on a murky 27 April 1987, passing Worting Junction near Basingstoke with the 09.00 Bournemouth-Waterloo. Both: *Author*

The Electro-Diesels

Above: One of the most unusual workings recorded for 'JA' No 73001 was on 1 March 1992, when it piloted Class 20s Nos 20121 and 20117 on a 'DC Tours' special from Yeovil Junction to Waterloo. The train is seen near Tisbury with its most unusual threesome on the front. *Brian Beer*

Below: Mainline Freight blue-liveried No 73114 *Stewarts Lane Traction Maintenance Depot*, departs from the 'up loop' at Clapham Junction with a Mk2 test train from Eastleigh Works to Clapham Junction yard on 30 April 1997. The Mk2s had just been refurbished at Eastleigh Works and required a full test before returning to traffic on the Anglia main line. *Brian Morrison*

In traffic - Central Section

Above: Until 1983 the daily Chessington/Tolworth to Acton coal empties operated via Wimbledon, Streatham and Wandsworth to reach Clapham Junction and then the West London Extension Railway via Kensington Olympia. However, between 1983 and January 1987 the train worked via Wimbledon and East Putney to reach Clapham Junction. No 73128 passes Clapham Junction (Central) on 24 April 1981 with the 09.55 Wimbledon West Yard-Acton coal empties. *Author*

Left: The operation of Freightliner trains by electro-diesels has always been unusual. One train which did infrequently see Class 73s on Freightliner wagons was the Seaford service which operated in the early 1980s from Willesden in north London to the Sussex town. A southbound container train bound for Seaford from Willesden passes Clapham Junction on 14 May 1983. *Brian Morrison*

Above: With the now closed gantry-mounted West London Junction signal box on the horizon, No 73141 descends the Pouparts Junction-Longhedge Junction spur on 28 March 1980, with a mixed freight bound for Battersea yard from Three Bridges. *Author*

Right: Coal traffic to the distribution heads at Tolworth and Chessington was usually transported in hoppers for easy discharge at the sites. However, on occasions coal box wagons were used, requiring grab discharge and a sweep out. A rake of 17 unfitted coal wagons and a brake van on the rear approaches Clapham Junction (Central) on 15 August 1973 *en route* from Wimbledon West yard to Acton via Streatham. This was one of the few workings which took a Class 74 off the South Western Division. *Brian Morrison*

Right: Privately-owned aggregate trains were and indeed still are a regular sight on the Central Section tracks, operating to/from off-loading points at Purley, and Salfords. In more recent years traction has been provided by Classes 37, 60 privately-owned Class 59s or 66s. However, on 3 November 1984 'more yellow'-liveried No 73126 approaches Norbury with the 10.23 Salfords-Brett Marine (Hoo Junction), formed of nine empty private-owner bogie hoppers. *Author*

Left: The use of EDs on the Southern Region-Western Region coal duties was always somewhat surprising, considering that only 600hp was available over the arduous, then non-electrified West London Extension tracks, but the locomotives always seemed to cope. No 73124 approaches Clapham Junction (Central) on 5 March 1981 with an Acton-bound service. *Author*

Right: The Southern Region, then Network SouthEast Central Division's and latterly Connex South Central and now Southern's main EMU servicing and maintenance facility is located at Selhurst. Up until the late 1980s, in addition to EMU stock, a number of locomotive-hauled vehicles were also maintained at the depot. Executive-liveried No 73127 attaches to a BSK and TSO in the yard on 30 May 1985 before departing for Clapham Junction. *Author*

Above: Often the daily Brett Marine-Purley/Salfords aggregate train produced a pair of Class 73s during the mid-1980s, and on a number of occasions two Class 73/0s were used. On 30 August 1984 the Brett-Salfords train, headed by Nos 73002 and 73003, is seen passing the splendid semaphore signal gantry at Redhill which, alas, has now been removed. *Author*

Below: NSE-liveried No 73133 *The Bluebell Railway* passes through the engine run-round crossing between platforms 12 and 13 at London Bridge (Central) on 8 September 1992 prior to working an observation car special to East Grinstead, marking the handover of Hill Place Viaduct from BR to the Bluebell Railway. *Author*

With one Southern Railway, and two British Rail-designed utility vans as a load, 'more yellow'-liveried No 73138 approaches Horley on 30 August 1984 with an afternoon van train from Redhill to Brighton. Unfortunately the driver has selected two white blanks as the train's route indication rather than the two-character route display. *Author*

Above: Making a more pleasing picture than the conventional front three-quarter view, is this study of 'more yellow' liveried No 73131 approaching Balcombe on 16 June 1984 with the Brighton-New Cross Gate empty newspaper van train, formed of a mixture of BR and ex-Southern types. *Michael J. Collins*

Right: The countryside to the north of Brighton, and in particular around Patcham, provides some very pleasant photographic locations. In this deep tree-lined cutting near Patcham Tunnel, No 73102 hauls a short van train bound for Brighton on 28 August 1982. *Author*

Left and Below: On 28 April 1982 the restored VSOE Pullman train made its first public working over the then BR network, when it was chartered from London to Brighton and return, forming the 'Brighton Festival Belle'. Motive power on the outward journey was provided by No 73101 *Brighton Evening Argus,* and in the illustration left is seen passing Keymer Junction, near Wivelsfield. Due to electric train heat problems, the return service was double-headed by No 73142 *Broadlands* (coupled inside), and the duo are seen in the lower plate with the splendid Pullman rake near Patcham Tunnel. Both: *Author*

Above: For several years in the late 1970s/early 1980s, regular stone services worked between Lavant Quarry, and Drayton gravel terminal on the coastway line. These were usually operated by Class 73s and formed of large Francis Parker side-discharge bogie hoppers. On 13 May 1981, one of these trains is seen approaching Chichester, headed by No 73004. *Les Bertram*

Right: East Grinstead is a location which did not see '73' action every day, especially with two observation saloons. On 8 September 1992, NSE SouthCentral signed over Hill Place Viaduct to the Bluebell Railway to assist their plans to extend the line to East Grinstead. To take guests to this event, NSE-liveried No 73133 *The Bluebell Railway,* plus observation saloons Nos 9004 and 975025 formed a special from London Bridge. The train is seen at East Grinstead. *Author*

Above: A regular ED diagram on the 'Coastway' route for many years was the daily Fratton-Hove pick-up freight, which normally conveyed coal and fuel oil. On 6 October 1983 the train was headed by No 73121 *Croydon 1883-1983* and is seen passing Angmering *en route* for Hove. *John Vaughan*

Left: Displaying Pullman livery, No 73101 *The Royal Alex'* poses at Brighton with the VSOE VIP train stock on 2 May 1992, forming a charter special to Victoria, immediately following its re-naming from *Brighton Evening Argus. Author*

Above: The British portion of the 'Night Ferry 'service was a regular Class 73 duty after the demise of the Class 71s in 1977, until the overnight service stopped running in 1980. On 22 July 1979 No 73141 is seen at the head of the southbound train awaiting departure from Victoria. *Brian Morrison*

Below: The 'Night Ferry' train was unique in that it operated over UK tracks with French (SNCF) passenger rolling stock, which arrived and departed from England via the Dover train ferry. On 16 August 1980, No 73139 approaches Shortlands with the up service formed of two SNCF vans, four SNCF coaches and the required BR brake vehicle on the rear. *Brian Beer*

In traffic - Eastern Section

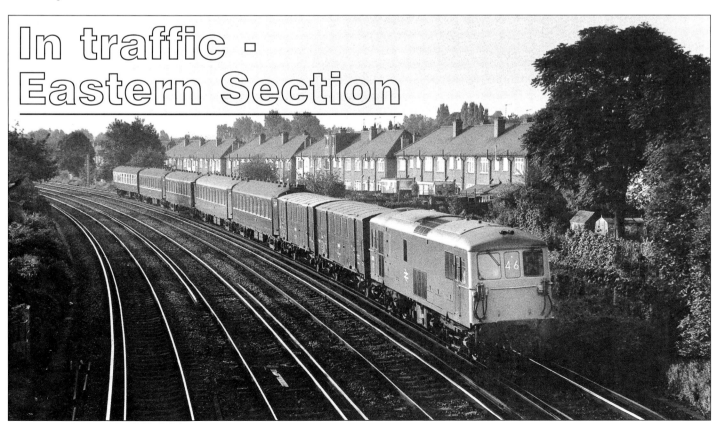

Above: With the introduction of new liveries on the Class 73s in the 1980s and 1990s, many trains with locomotives painted in mixed liveries were to be found. No 73108 in 'Dutch' yellow and grey colours and No 73133 in Network SouthEast livery pass Wandsworth Road with an engineers' train from Woking to Hoo Junction on 16 December 1993. *Author*

Left: 'More yellow'-liveried No 73105 hauls empty Brett Aggregate bogie hoppers through Denmark Hill on 12 September 1984 bound for the Brett private sidings on the Isle of Grain. *Author*

Right: Unfortunately one does not see many 'pick-up' type goods trains today. However, in the 1960s many such services were found, and one headed by No E6044, later No 73202, is seen on 1 October 1968 at Petts Wood. *John Cooper-Smith*

Above: Emerging from the southern portal of Chislehurst Tunnel and approaching Elmstead Woods, ED No 73140 heads a Hither Green Sidings-Ore permanent way train on 16 May 1974. Note the screw coupling hanging on the front drawhook, which should have been replaced in the engine room after its previous use. *Brian Morrison*

Above: With the tower blocks and station of Lewisham as a backdrop, a pair of Class 73/1s, No 73104 and 73123 *Gatwick Express* head a long MGR train through the station on 28 July 1986 bound for Ridham Dock. *Brian Beer*

Left: There are few weeks in the year when the VSOE is not involved in some sort of charter work, to bring its owners, Sea Containers, additional revenue. On 27 July 1984 the set, headed by No 73140, operated a special from Victoria to Harrietsham, and is seen approaching Swanley. *Brian Morrison*

Above: One of the major innovations in ballast transport and delivery to engineering sites in the 1990s was delivery of the self-discharge 'Skako' train. This train is seen in Hoo Junction Yard on 1 February 1993, powered by 'Dutch'-liveried Class 73/1 No 73138. When this picture was taken the 'Skako' train had not entered revenue service and was still undergoing tests. In more recent years a number of purpose-built Network Rail self-discharge ballast trains have entered service. *Author*

Right: Looking rather weather-worn, NSE-liveried Class 73/1 No 73136 *Kent Youth Music* hauls a loaded spoil train through Higham on 1 February 1993 *en route* from the nearby Hoo Junction Yard to Ashford. *Author*

Below: Two Class 73/1s, No 73114 in Main Line livery and 73107 in 'Dutch' pose with an engineers train at Appledore on the Ashford-Hastings line on 18 April 1992. The train was involved in a weekend-long relaying possession between Ashford and Appledore. *Brian Morrison*

Above: To supply material for the building of flyover supports at Gloucester Road Junction near East Croydon in 1983, regular trains of coal slag were operated from Betteshanger Colliery, formed of 30 MTV wagons powered by pairs of Class 73s. On 23 June 1983, one of these trains, headed by Nos 73108 and 73136, is seen passing Paddock Wood. *Author*

Left: Network SouthEast-liveried No 73126 *Kent and East Sussex Railway* stands at Cannon Street on 27 March 1992 with an officers' inspection special which worked throughout the soon-to-be-formed 'Networker' area of Kent. On the right is Class 415 4EPB unit No 5159 stabled during the off-peak period. *Author*

Right: The nightly Dover-Manchester Travelling Post Office train was a regular Class 73 duty for many years. The service was eventually withdrawn in 2003 when Royal Mail decreed that the price charged by EWS for operating Mail trains was excessive. On 30 July 1996, the 19.20 departure from Dover bound for Manchester is seen near Westenhanger powered by 'Dutch'-liveried No 73107 *Redhill 1944-1994*. *Author*

Above: No 73139 takes the Herne Bay line at Faversham on 26 September 1982 hauling 400 tons of new track ballast to a weekend engineering site near Herne Bay. Although the live rail is present, the pick-up shoes are in the raised position, indicating the locomotive was being operated under diesel conditions. *Author*

Above: For a number of years the RTC Derby-based track recording trains were powered by Class 73s when working on former Southern Region metals. In the 1990s this frequently saw the use of 'top and tail' Class 73s working either end of three or four departmental vehicles. On 7 April 1997, the High Speed Track Recording Coach No DB999550 is seen as the third vehicle from the front of this Stewarts Lane to Stewarts Lane via Maidstone, Dover and Ashford run powered by ED Nos 73128 and 73119.
Brian Morrison

Left: Deputising for the usual DEMU, Class 73/1s No 73110 and 73104 'top and tail' a diagram on the Ashford-Hastings 'Marsh Line' route on 1 May 1995, passenger accommodation being provided by 4CEP No 1612. Here the train led by No 73110 arrives at Rye forming the 09.22 Ashford-Hastings.
Brian Morrison

Above: Passing Hawkesbury Street Junction signalbox, Dover, a pair of Class 73/1s, No 73134 *Woking Homes 1885-1985* and No 73105 power the 11.00 Hoo Junction-Folkestone West engineers train on 2 March 1996. *Brian Morrison*

Below: A view which is slightly different today. This was the view on 16 November 1991 of what is now Dollands Moor, near the UK entrance to the Channel Tunnel. At this time the ground for the yard had been prepared but apart from the down loop and one siding nothing had been built. Pioneer ED No E6001 shunts three breakdown recovery vehicles while privately-owned Class 20s Nos 20138/087 are attached to the rear. *Brian Morrison*

In traffic - On Foreign Metals

Above: Until its closure to general freight traffic in 1983, Acton Yard on the Western Region was a regular haunt for EDs on light weight coal duties, mainly working to Tolworth and Chessington. Traversing the up relief line at Acton Main Line, No 73112 hauls the Acton-Tolworth coal on 1 June 1981. *Author*

Left: No, this is not a wrong picture for a book on electro-diesels, but shows the versatility of the fleet. On 3 January 2005 'Hampshire' units No. 205028/032 were hauled from Tonbridge to Meldon Quarry and as the Class 66 rostered for the move did not have high-level air connection, GBRf No 73204 was used as a coupling translator. The train is seen near Cowley Bridge, Exeter. *Author*

Above: Using every bit of the 1,200hp available from their auxiliary diesel engines, Nos 73107 and 73130 haul a heavy empty powdered-cement train out of South West sidings, Willesden on 11 May 1984, bound for Southampton. *Author*

Right and Below: Probably the most unusual ED working of 1981 took place on 14 May when the Derby-based High Speed Track Recording Coach No DB999550 was operated with ED No 73103, Class 414 (2HAP) No 6103 and Class 33 No 33112 from Salisbury to Exeter and return; this was the first Class 73/HAP working into Devon. The picture right shows the train at Exeter St Davids with two bemused staff looking on, while the view below shows the train departing St Davids and up the incline towards Exeter Central. Both: *Charles Beatson*

Special Duties

Above: Southern Region internally-worked Royal trains were for many years Class 73-operated, and after its naming in September 1980 No 73142 (73201) *Broadlands* was the firm favourite. A Royal Train on 5 June 1984 conveying HM The Queen to Havant is seen approaching New Malden. Note the locomotive number positioned under the nameplate, a livery variant only carried for a short period. *Author*

Left: After the wedding of HRH The Prince of Wales and Lady Diana Spencer on 29 July 1981, a Royal Wedding train was operated, conveying the Prince and Princess to Romsey on the first stage of their honeymoon at Broadlands. The Royal Special, headed by No 73142 *Broadlands*, was formed of a Mk2 FO, Mk1 BCK and the SR General Manager's Saloon No DB975025, the latter carrying the happy couple. The train is seen approaching Clapham Cutting with a suitable headcode. *Brian Morrison*

Above: Another special ED train was operated on 28 May 1982 when Pope John Paul II arrived for a visit to Great Britain, and was conveyed by train from Gatwick Airport to London Victoria, motive power being provided by 'Royal' No 73142. The train passes through Clapham Cutting carrying an appropriate HF (Holy Father) headcode. As with the Wedding train, the guest was conveyed in the SR General Manager's Saloon, in this case coupled directly behind the locomotive. *Brian Morrison*

Right: On several occasions EDs have been requested for railtour operations. One tour utilised two Class 73s, sandwiching two Class 491 (4TC) units, was the Southern Electric Group's 'JA Jamboree' operated on 17 March 1984 from Waterloo to Waterloo via Chessington, Shepperton, Reading and Southampton. The train, headed by No 73126 displaying an 'unusual' but appropriate headcode for the author, poses at Chessington South. No 73138 was coupled at the rear of the train. *Author*

Left: The annual weed-control operation often took locomotive-hauled specials to unusual lines and areas, some of which did not usually see locomotives very often. On 17 May 1986 'more yellow'-liveried Class 73/1 No 73140 powered the Chipmans weed-control train to the London terminal of Holborn Viaduct, and is shown approaching Elephant & Castle station carrying a suitable 'CC' headcode. *Brian Morrison*

Right: For the summer diesel gala on the Paignton & Dartmouth Railway over the weekend of 19/20 June 1993, Network SouthEast provided two Class 73/1s to work services over the railway. The locomotives selected were Nos 73109 *Battle of Britain - 50th Anniversary* and 73101 *The Royal Alex'*. The pair, led by No 73101, head a four-coach GWR-liveried train away from Churston towards Kingswear on 19 June. *Author*

Left: Between 1989 and 1994 Class 73/2 No 73205 *London Chamber of Commerce* was allocated to European Passenger Services for 'Eurostar' traction development work. It was used as a power source for test trains, and received some structural modifications for this work. For most of the time it was semi-permanently coupled to former Class 33/1 No 33115, which was rebuilt as a power collection test vehicle for Eurostar power cars and renumbered as hauled vehicle No 83301. The pair usually operated with a 6TC formation. The unusual test train is seen arriving at Waterloo on 5 February 1992. *Brian Morrison*

Above: In mid-1993 three Class 73/0s, Nos 73001, 73002 and 73005 were transferred from Stewarts Lane to Birkenhead North for use on the MerseyRail electric network for powering engineers trains. No 73006 followed later in the year. The class's first outing on a passenger train in the North West was on 12 March 1994 when Nos 73006 and 73002 powered 'The Jolly JAs' railtour from Chester to Llandudno Junction. The two locomotives are seen at Llandudno Junction, with No 73006 displaying the yellow and brown MerseyRail livery applied just prior to the tour. *Chris Dixon*

Below: The unusual sight of Gatwick Express stock and a Class 73/2 at St Pancras Station turned many people's heads on 29 April 1996. The train was brought into St Pancras as part of the franchise handover of Midland Main Line and Gatwick Express to National Express Group. Parked in the non-platform centre road, Class 73/2s Nos 73205 and 73210 'top and tail' a rake of five Class 488 vehicles. *Brian Morrison*

Channel Tunnel Duties

On 20 June 1993 the first 'Eurostar' Class 373 set, No PS1 (3001/02) arrived in England through the Channel Tunnel. To haul the set to North Pole International Depot, Class 73s Nos 73118 and 73205 with power-collection test vehicle No 83301 were used. The locomotives, complete with match vehicles, are seen coupling up to the 'Eurostar' set on the International Main Line at the Eurotunnel site at Cheriton. On the right SNCF 68xxx class No 68041 is seen; this locomotive hauled the 'Eurostar' set through the Channel Tunnel. *Author*

Right: As dawn rises on 13 July 1993, Eurostar set No PS1 is hauled through Shortlands sandwiched by EDs Nos 73105 and 73118 *en route* from Maidstone to North Pole Depot. For several weeks after delivery, Pre-Service 1 (PS1) was not authorised to operate under its own power, and ED 'tractors' were used for all moves. *Brian Morrison*

Below: EPS-operated ED No 73130 stands at Waterloo International on 1 February 1995 hauling Class 92 No 92020 *Milton,* which had just been handed over to European Passenger Services after construction by Brush Traction. Eurostar Class 373 sets are seen stabled in platforms 21 to 23 prior to forming international departures to Paris and Brussels. *Author*

Left: After the first 'Eurostar' was delivered to European Passenger Services, the train was not initially authorised to operate under its own power unless an engineering occupation was taken. To move the shortened train to and from the main test site situated between Dollands Moor and Ashford, a pair of Class 73s were used. On 14 August 1993, Nos 73118 and 73130 haul 'Eurostar' set PS1 through Kensington Olympia *en route* to Dollands Moor. *Chris Wilson*

Above: The first time a full 20-car 'Eurostar' set United Kingdom 1 or UK1 for short ventured onto the main line was on 23 November 1993 when it was hauled by Class 73s Nos 73118 *The Romney Hythe & Dymchurch Railway* and 73126 *Kent & East Sussex Railway*. Coupled in front and behind the Class 73s were recently-introduced coupling match wagons, converted from van stock and fitted with drop-head Scharfenberg couplers. This most unusual combination with a wagon leading a train is pictured at Bromley South, while heading from North Pole International Depot to Dollands Moor, from where active testing was to take place. *Brian Morrison*

Above: No 73130 with its 'Eurostar' Scharfenberg coupling in the raised position, stands at North Pole International Depot, with two £24m 'Eurostar' sets in adjacent stabling sidings. No 73130 shares duties with No 73118 based at North Pole International Depot. Apart from depot shunting, the locomotives operate over the main line if required. *Author*

Right: During 1993 and 1994 Class 73s coupled with 'Eurostar' coupling translator wagons at either end were a regular sight on the West London Line and the route between London and the Channel Tunnel, shadowing Class 373 'Eurostar' sets until technical equipment was deemed as 'safe' for operation without the risk of failure. For the Channel Tunnel Royal opening on 6 May 1994, as a 'belt and braces' measure the 'Eurostar rescue' train operated in front of the Royal special. It is seen here formed of two coupling adaptor wagons with Class 73s Nos 73132 and 73128 in the middle near Polhill Tunnel. *Author*

Above and Left: After various Class 73s from the core fleet were used, European Passenger Services were eventually allocated two locomotives of their own, Nos 73118 and 73130. Both were heavily modified by Adtranz Crewe and fitted with drophead Scharfenberg couplers, to enable direct attachment to Eurostar stock and obviate the need for barrier wagons. The rebuilt work was extensive and included a new detachable front end module attached to the former buffer stocks. The new coupler also retained conventional coupling hooks, air pipe connections and multiple control equipment, and above all, a headlight. Although the locomotives could be 'close-coupled' with a conventional screw coupling, frequently the pair operate in multiple using their drophead Scharfenberg couplers, as shown in these views of the pair at North Pole International Depot in 2003. Both: *Author*

Right: The Network Rail/Serco track test train visited South West Trains suburban lines out of Waterloo on 3 March 2003, and as a pair of EWS-operated Class 73s were not available, No 73130 was hired from European Passenger Services. The unusual ED visitor is seen travelling over the Strawberry Hill-Shepperton branch, trailing a five-car track test formation led by EWS ED No 73131. A Class 455 is seen passing with a Shepperton-Waterloo service. *Paul Davis*

Below: One of the most unusual workings for the two European Passenger Services Class 73s came on 3 May 2001, when the two were sent light from North Pole Depot to Haywards Heath on hire to Virgin Trains to power the 14.18 Brighton-Manchester service, which started from Haywards Heath on that day due to the failure of the Class 47 on the train's inward working. The '73s' powered the service as far as Reading where this view of the train was taken. *Darren Ford*

GBRf Operations

Above: A naming ceremony with a difference took place at London Victoria on 12 October 2004. The four reinstated GBRf Class 73/2s were named *Alison* (73206), *Janice* (73204), *Jeanette* (73205) and *Lisa* (73209) after GBRf staff members. See the 'Game of the Name' chapter. After the namings, the EDs 'topped and tailed' a special train to Liverpool Street via Tonbridge, Redhill and the West London Line, seen awaiting departure from Victoria. *Darren Ford*

Below: Over the years we have seen some over-powered trains, but this might hold the record; four locomotives for four carriages! In connection with the naming of the four GBRf Class 73s at Victoria on 12 October 2004, all four 'topped and tailed' a special train from Victoria to Liverpool Street via Tonbridge and Redhill, recorded here at Tonbridge during a change direction move before heading to Redhill and London. *Brian Morrison*

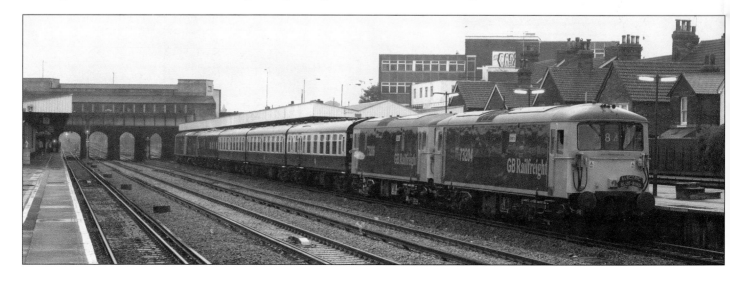

The Electro-Diesels

Above: Deemed by GBRf as the 'Electric Blue-birds', the Class 73/2 EDs commenced engineering train operations on 2/3 July 2004 when Nos 73204 and 73205 flanked Fragonset Type 3 No 33103 powering an Eastleigh Yard-Hounslow Junction ballast train formed of Network Rail 'Falcon' wagons. Complete with an 'Electric Blue-bird' headboard, the return working to Eastleigh passes near Egham. *Kim Fullbrook*

Below: Previously Gatwick Express locomotives named *Stewarts Lane 1860-1985* and *London Chamber of Commerce* respectively, GBRf Nos 73205 and 73204 approach Orpington on 15 September 2004, hauling a driver-training special formed of autoballaster wagons as the 12.45 Hoo Junction to Tonbridge West Yard via Dartford, Sidcup, Lee Spur, Sevenoaks, Ashford, Dover and Canterbury. *Brian Morrison*

Above: The use of GBRf Class 73/2s on Network Rail ballast trains slowly increased in early 2005 with additional contracts being executed. On 15 May 2005, No 73205 *Jeanette* stands in the early morning sun at London Bridge (Central side) with a rake of Network Rail 'Autoballaster' hoppers. *Graham Vickers*

Below: On 19 September 2005, GBRailfreight deployed Class 73/2 Nos 73209 *Alison* and 73206 *Lisa* to transfer two Network Rail vehicles from York to Hither Green. The locomotives arrived in York the previous day, after attending the Nene Valley Railway Diesel Gala. Minor problems occurred at York when EWS was unable to provide groundstaff to man York yard, to allow the locomotives to attach to the train. The ensemble departed York around 17.00, over four hours late, and is recorded south of Colton Junction on the East Coast main line heading for Peterborough, where it recessed overnight. *Richard Tuplin*

Right: In the days of British Rail, it would have been unheard of for a Class 73 to be stabled at York, some 200 miles from the nearest 750V dc third rail! However, under the privatised banner, like most classes of modern traction locomotive, the '73' have been, and indeed still are, recorded all over the country. No 73209 *Alison* is seen stabled in the station sidings at York on 19 September 2005, prior to powering the engineers train to Peterborough illustrated on the adjacent page. *Ron Cover*

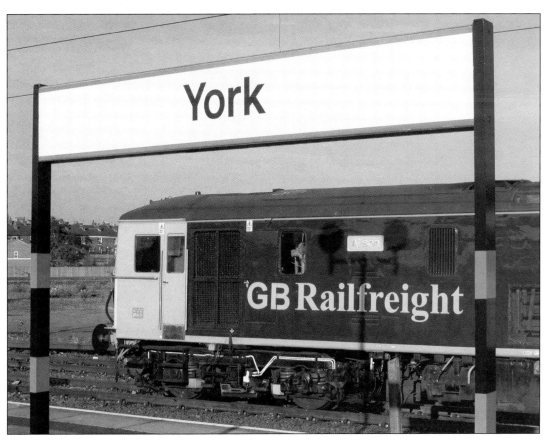

Below: One of the rarest workings for a GBRf Class 73/2 in 2005 was on 2 November, when Nos 73204 and 73206 were used as coupling adaptors to a GNER HST set being transferred from GNER to FGW. The coaching stock, 'top and tailed' by the EDs and powered by Class 66/7 No 66717, passes Aller, west of Newton Abbot. *Sam Felce*

Above: GBRf have been very supportive of the railway enthusiasts since commencing operation with Class 73s, making examples available to light railways for gala events. Nos 73206 and 73209 visited the Nene Valley Railway at Peterborough over the weekend of 17/18 September 2005 and powered passenger services formed of foreign stock. One such train is seen approaching Wansford and about to cross the River Nene from Peterborough on 17 September. *Darren Ford*

Left: GBRf-operated, Gatwick Express-liveried No 73208 pilots GBRf No 73209 through Havant on 28 January 2006, forming the 12.40 Hove-Eastleigh engineers train. No 73208 was taken 'off-lease' with Gatwick Express in mid-2005 and in spring 2006 awaited repainting. *Mark Pike*

Above: Over the weekend of 7/8 May 2005 the West Somerset Railway held their annual diesel gala event and GBRf supplied three Class 73/2s. Here on 7 May Nos 73204 and 73209 pass through Turks Cutting between Crowcombe Heathfield and Stogumber, with a Bishops Lydeard-bound train from Minehead. On the rear of the train, out of view, is No 73205. *Brian Garrett*

Right: No 73205 is seen leading a Bishops Lydeard-Minehead train at Woolsten Moor, located between Stogumber and Williton. Locomotives Nos 73204 and 73209 are coupled on the rear. For the WSR gala event, the locomotives arrived on the line on 5 May running as the 07.17 Tonbridge Yard to Bishops Lydeard. *Brian Garrett*

Return to the Main Line

Above: Shepherd Neame's 'The Spitfire' charter on 4 September 2005 operated from London Bridge to Sheerness-on-Sea via Ramsgate and Margate, behind 'Black 5' 4-6-0 No 45231 *Sherwood Forester*, where Fragonset-liveried Class 73/1 No 73107 *Spitfire* took over to Faversham, the 'Black 5' being used again for the return run to London Bridge via Dover Priory. Departing from Sheerness, the electro-diesel makes its way off the Isle of Sheppey back to the main line and approaches Queenborough. No 73107 is the only operational FM Rail-owned Class 73 and was returned to front-line use after a major overhaul at the RTC, Derby. *Brian Morrison*

Above: The two Network Rail-liveried Class 73/2s, Nos 73213 and 73212, were returned from FM Rail Derby to the south following overhaul early in November 2005. As a recertification test for third-rail operation the pair, in multiple with FM Rail-owned, Fragonset-liveried Class 73/1 No 73107 powered a 'running in' special on 15 November 2005, formed of the 'Queen of Scots' Pullman train running as the 09.30 from Clapham Junction to Tonbridge Yard via Sevington. The unique combination is seen near Charing, Kent. *Brian Morrison*

Below: The arctic weather conditions in East Kent on 28 December 2005 saw a number of Electrostar-formed services trapped by iced-up third rails, especially in the Ashford-Dover area. The two Network Rail-liveried Class 73s, Nos 73212/213, were sent to assist the 04.43 Dover Priory-Victoria service but became trapped soon after departing from Folkestone Central. Eventually two of the GBRf locomotives, Nos 73204/209, assisted the train into Ashford station. The quadruple-headed train is seen passing the Balfour Beatty plant works at Ashford. *Mark Horton*

Above: The South West Trains 'Thunderbird' Class 73s, of which there are now three, Nos 73109, 73201 and 73235, are always an attraction for enthusiasts. On 16 April 2005, some services between Waterloo and Alton were powered by No 73109 *Battle of Britain 50th Anniversary*, coupled at the west end of 4CIG No 1398 and 4VEP No 3481. The 11.53 Waterloo-Alton service is seen rounding the curve at Badshot Lea near Farnham. *Ken Brunt*

Left: On 18 May 2004, SWT 'Thunderbird' No 73109 *Battle of Britain 50th Anniversary* was used to haul failed 1963-design EMUs 4CIG No 1316 and 4VEP No 3431 from Basingstoke to East Wimbledon depot. The train is seen traversing the 'up' slow line at New Malden, the driver choosing to display two white blanks in place of the booked headcode 34. *Tony Rispoli*

Right: Carrying full SWT livery, 'Thunderbird' No 73109 was out and about on 1 March 2005, running light from Woking to Bournemouth to collect defective Class 421/8 4CIG No (42)1392 and haul it to East Wimbledon Depot. The train is shown passing through Oatlands Cutting, between Weybridge and Walton-on-Thames. *Chris Nevard*

Below: No 73109 *Battle of Britain 50th Anniversary*, operating under diesel conditions by the plume of smoke above, is seen on 6 January 2005 at Basingstoke powering an empty stock move to East Wimbledon Depot, after a defect was found on a 1963-design unit on a southbound service. *Jon Harding*

Above: South West Trains started to repaint their 'Thunderbird' locomotives in 'Desiro' style in spring 2005. No 73235 was used for driver training in April 2005 between Poole and Eastleigh, to increase the number of drivers able to work the locomotives. On 15 April 2005, No 73235 propels Class 442 set No 2423 through Millbrook with an Eastleigh-Poole training special. *Mark V. Pike*

Below: No 73109 *Battle of Britain 50th Anniversary* emerged from East Wimbledon Depot painted in SWT Desiro colours in late May 2005. On 1 June 2005 it was used to haul the 09.52 Bournemouth West Depot to Wimbledon Depot scrap stock move, consisting of 4VEP set No 3536 and 4CIG sets Nos 1398 and 1396. The transit move is recorded passing Branksome. *Mark V. Pike*

On Preserved Lines

Above: For the 25 June 1996 diesel gala event held on the Torbay & Dartmouth Railway between Paignton and Kingswear, Mainline Freight loaned aircraft blue-liveried No 73133 *The Bluebell Railway* to the line. For safety reasons the locomotive was driven by a Mainline Freight driver with a TDR route conductor. The locomotive was used to power both freight and passenger turns. It is seen passing the long-closed Goodrington signalbox powering the 18.20 demonstration ballast train from Paignton Queens Park to Churston. *Author*

Right: With just four Mk1 and former DMU passenger cars as its load, No 73133 passes the picturesque Waterside between Churston and Goodrington forming the 11.40 Kingswear-Paignton Queens Park local service on 25 June 1996. *Author*

Left: Returned to 1960s electric-blue livery with small yellow warning panels, No E6005 was working on the Severn Valley Railway during 2005. It was originally taken to the line to assist in line engineering work but was then used during the year's diesel gala event. It is seen arriving at Arley. *Darren Ford*

Right: The number of Class 73s that have been returned to operational condition on light railways following withdrawal by EWS is quite amazing. No 73129, the original *City of Winchester*, still painted in Network SouthEast livery is now used on the Gloucester-Warwickshire Railway. On 5 November 2005 the locomotive, with a five-vehicle Mk1 formation, is seen near Didbrook. *John Wills*

Right: In preservation, No 73138 has been returned to 'large logo' blue livery, as sported by the fleet in the 1980s. Restoration has been carried out at Barrow Hill, and during 2005 it attended display events at Crewe Locomotive Works and Norwich. The locomotive is fully operational and in 2006 is scheduled to take part in demonstration running on the Barrow Hill Roundhouse display track. It is seen at Crewe Works on 10 September 2005. *Darren Ford*

Left: Mainline Freight-liveried No 73133 *The Bluebell Railway* was modified by Stewarts Lane for driver's route training. The headcode boxes were removed and extra seating provided. To provide front-end indication, Group Standard light clusters were added, making the locomotive immediately identifiable. No 73133 is now preserved on the Vale of Glamorgan Railway, but is seen here at Rawtenstall on the East Lancs Railway on 6 July 2002. *Darren Ford*

Right: A view taken during the 2005 Great Central Railway diesel gala weekend shows ED No 73003 (E6003) arriving at Loughborough from Leicester formed of Class 421 4CIG No 1393 and Class 33 No 33117 on the rear. In the background, the line's preserved Class 25, No D5185, performs shunting work. *Brian Garrett*

For the summer diesel gala on the Paignton & Dartmouth Railway on 19/20 June 1993, NSE provided two Class 73/1s to operate on the line. The locomotives selected were Network SouthEast-liveried No 73109 *Battle of Britain - 50th Anniversary* and Pullman-liveried No 73101 *The Royal Alex'*. No 73109 pilots No 73101 with a seven-car formation past Waterside with a Kingswear-Paignton service. *Author*